THEY CALL US DEAD MEN

REFLECTIONS ON LIFE AND CONSCIENCE

They Call Us Dead Men

REFLECTIONS ON LIFE AND CONSCIENCE

DANIEL BERRIGAN, s.j.

INTRODUCTION BY
WILLIAM STRINGFELLOW

The Macmillan Company, New York

Collier-Macmillan Limited, London

MS: Catholic Church

FIRST MACMILLAN PAPERBACK EDITION 1968

The Macmillan Company, New York
Collier-Macmillan Canada Ltd., Toronto, Ontario
Library of Congress catalog card number: 66-11689
Printed in the United States of America

ACKNOWLEDGMENTS

Some of the material in this book was originally published, in
somewhat different form, elsewhere: "St. Paul: Figure of Crisis,"
published under the title "St. Paul and the Crisis of Christians,"
Perspectives, November-December, 1962; "Notes on Renewal," *Grail
International Review*, Vol. VI, No. 3; "The Eternal Youth of the
Church," reprinted with the permission of the *Liturgical Conference*,
from their Proceedings of the 1962 Liturgical Week; "Sacred Art
and the Life of Man," *Worship;* "Man's Spirit and Technology,"
Fellowship, May, 1965, Vol. 31, No. 5, and *World View*, November,
1965.

Quoted material appearing in the book was used with the permission of the following: Alfred A. Knopf, Inc., for *The Collected
Tales of E. M. Forster;* and A. Watkins, Inc., for *Descent Into Hell*
by Charles Williams, copyright 1937 Charles Williams, copyright
1949 Pelligrini and Cudahy. The quotation that precedes the Introduction is taken from La Bible de Jérusalem.

Imprimi potest
John McGinty, S.J.
May 15, 1965
Nihil obstat
Daniel V. Flynn, J.C.D.
Censor Librorum
Imprimatur
✠ Terence J. Cooke, D.D., V.G.
Vicar General

December 17, 1965

The nihil obstat and imprimatur are official declarations that a
book or pamphlet is free of doctrinal or moral error. No implication
is contained therein that those who have granted the nihil obstat and
imprimatur agree with the contents, opinions, or statements expressed.

To
Jim and Sally Douglass

Peacemaking is hard
hard almost as war.
The difference being one
we can stake life upon
and limb and thought and love.

I stake this poem out
dead man to a dead stick
to tempt an Easter chance—
if faith may be
truth, an evil chance
penultimate at last,

not last. We are not lost.

When these lines gathered
of no resource at all
serenity and strength,
it dawned on me—

a man stood on his nails

an ash like dew, a sweat
smelling of death and life.
Our evil Friday fled,
the blind face gently turned
another way, toward life

a man walks in his shroud

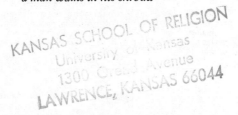

Contents

"Tenus . . . pour gens qui vont mourir, et nous voilà vivants" (2 Cor. 6:8–9).

Introduction

*So shall we all at last attain to the unity inherent in our faith
and our knowledge of the Son of God—to mature manhood,
measured by nothing less than the full stature of Christ. We
are no longer to be children, tossed by the waves and whirled
about by every fresh gust of teaching, dupes of crafty rogues
and their deceitful schemes. No, let us speak the truth in
love; so shall we fully grow up into Christ.*

Ephesians 4:13-15

THIS PASSIONATE ONE, this meek poet, this exemplary human
being, this priest of Christ now gives us a wise,
lucid, compelling and edifying testament affirming the
sacramental integrity of human life in this world.

It goes without saying that this is *not* a religious book,
though, I suspect, it is likely to be catalogued as such. If
the librarians and book editors classify it in that way it
will be a grotesque mistake. Few, if any, religious books
are about Jesus Christ since few religious books are about
what it means to be a mature human being in this world. I
can recollect no religious book which is concerned, truth-
fully, with that style of life in Christ in this world which
authorizes and constitutes the most profoundly human life.
If this is considered a religious book, that will be misfor-
tune, because those who might be emancipated by it and
many who would simply rejoice in it will not find it.

The book is not religious in the conventional sense of
that term: it does not expound dogma; it does not resort
to jargon; it upholds no ritualistic vanities; it is not argu-
mentative about religious ideas; it advocates no pietism
of any sort; it does not cater to the lust for indulgences; it
does not assault the conscience, nor does it insult intelligence.

The book is about life, not religion. It is about life in its
mundane aspects, here and now, in common history—art

[xi]

and work and leisure and technology and marriage and the traumas of social conflict. It is not about religion which, as Saint Paul so often admonished Christian people, always ends in idolatry, superstition, hallucination, or some similar discursion from life in this world.

This is a book about the sacramental integrity of human existence. It discerns that the drama of all time—which is the saga of death and resurrection, not, as the religious suppose, a conflict of evil and good—is impregnant in every and each event in this history: the trivial and the momentous, in the present day as much as long ago, for all human beings, not merely for an exclusive few, and, indeed, for all principalities and powers as well.

To become and be a mature human being, to be alive, in the midst of such a drama in which all men (whether they realize it or not) do in truth live, describes a radical participation. To be alive means, as Father Berrigan puts it, enduring "the crisis of grace." The fruit of the gift of Christ to this world is an unequivocal and utterly vulnerable immersion in the world as it is. It means an involvement innocent of either guile or prudence. It means confronting the withering, ingenious, redundant, bewildering and apparently inexhaustible assaults of death upon one's very being and upon the existence of everyone and everything else. It means living in such a way that life is welcomed as the extraordinary gift which life is and, then, honoring that gift by extravagance: by giving one's own life away. It means that sanctification—a life which is holy (that is, whole and fulfilled, not good or pure)—is the life expended in freedom from anxiety of death. Or, as Saint Paul once more reminds, it means living in this world by dying in Christ in this world.

It means that by the virtue of Christ the mature man in this world is a surrogate of all men.

Precisely this triumph of mature humanity in Jesus Christ gives veracity to the Gospel.

Father Berrigan now gives us a book which is a eucharist for that Gospel.

Saint Matthew's Day, 1965   WILLIAM STRINGFELLOW
New York City

THEY CALL US DEAD MEN

REFLECTIONS ON LIFE AND CONSCIENCE

1. Poverty and the Life of the Church

AN UNDERSTANDING OF human life must take into account, in the nature of things, both the person and the community. This is a truth not merely of biology or psychology; it is true of man's life in God as well. Moreover, a sense of the person and his community will also include a sense of the great events by which human history has taken shape. Creation, redemption, and the last day are the stages of an exodus and return that is the common destiny of all.

The laws of man's spiritual life, as his destiny goes forward, seem to be analogous to the laws of his biology. These latter laws, especially in light of the writings of Blondel, Bergson, and Teilhard de Chardin, are seen more and more today as symbols of the spiritual progress of man.

One aspect of this mysterious correspondence between nature and grace has to do with the subject of this chapter. First, the obvious facts. The organism of man, whether in its personal or social aspects, undergoes a development, marked by discernible stages. We note first a period of youth marked by a primitive, explosive, rather undisciplined and unaware life. Then follows a period of full development. The organism has become conscious, powerfully aware both of itself and of its world, imaginative, marked by a sense of responsibility toward man. Finally, a time of old age follows; its signs, in an extreme sense, include an enfeebled response to the energies of others, a sense of helplessness before the demands of life, especially as such demands are expressed in the curiosity and energy of the young.

Within social groupings, this latter stage also shows itself. It tends to stress the limiting aspects of experience; to warn the young, to see dangers in every situation. One notes also an amassing of norms and rules. Life tends to become more and more prudential and impersonal; a gradual dissolution of the unity between life and law seems to be the rule. Virtuous practice becomes a kind of protective encystment of men within their personal world instead of a leaven at work within the human community.

With regard to the Church, we note that the promise of Christ has assured her that she will know a perennial youth in this world; the biological cycle of man, which always includes death, will not touch her. This power of renewed youth, moreover, is not static or defenseless or useless. It is both a gift of the Holy Spirit and the sum of vitality of the organs and members of the Church, who in concert of action and adoration form her sacred *diakonia*.

However, in the light of Christ's promise (Mt. 28:20), it is by no means certain that each organ is promised what the whole organism is promised. To put the matter in another way, the youthfulness of the Church (viewed in her ideal redemptive condition: vital, aware, open to the world of man) is not simply an undisturbed continuous process. It is not as though the life of the Church were destined to go on, in an uninterrupted process of being and becoming, without crisis or war or defections or martyrdom. Neither can we realistically think that from time to time certain organs and members will not suffer replacement by more vigorous ones. Everything in Church history points to an opposite situation, in which the vitality of the Church was renewed by violent spasms of discontinuity, by the destruction of the old in favor of new stages of life. This remains so true, as a simple matter of history, that a disservice to the Church can be implied in the determination to cling to past forms and ways of thought simply because they were once noble and useful.

More nearly to our point, we might examine here the signs that point to the onset of organic senility in men of the Church. By way of analogy to biological life, one could note a hardening of tissues and organis that were designed, by their suppleness and adaptive power, to serve the entire organism. The arteries of youth, surely, are fitted to bear violent rhythms of contraction and expansion, rhythms that are always set in motion when a virile heart undertakes large tasks. A hardened artery, on the other hand, may have a certain advantage; it is impervious to outside dangers. But with respect to its task, it is less and less useful; and with respect to the good of the organism, it is a mortal danger.

Analogous to good health in a physical organism is the spirit of religious groups that are truly youthful. In them, everything is gently, simply, courageously in harmony. A few central realities have been hardily and imaginatively grasped, to the point where their assimilation colors and forms a view of life. Apparent oppositions are delicately held in suspension; action and contemplation, intelligence and passion, imagination and rational will, Christ and neighbor. Again, life energies are not dissipated in whim and mood. A controlled power is at command and can be brought to bear, with lucidity and appropriateness, on the point of need. In respect to their past, such groups are marked by an understanding that even good things can become useless as time goes on—certain methods of the apostolate, certain stresses on convention and rule—are best discarded when once they lose their usefulness.

Again, genuine youthfulness in the Church never can-
onizes human beings or their works. Among those in authority, there is a constant tendency not toward honors
and distinctions of place but toward a spirit of service.
Those who are subject to obedience hold their superiors in
reverence, without servility or formalism. The reality of
Christ is firmly grasped, in victory and combat, as the
only end of man's labor and hope, of the present life and
the end of things. In regard to the apostolate, youthful
minds sense that Christianity must begin its task in the
world by first cleansing its own dwelling. And among the
things to be cleansed are surely the detritus of dead categories, inert truths, feeble devotional symbols, curial rhetoric, fear of the world, hatred of modern life—all the dead
methods and formulas that suffocate larger issues of life
and process, an unhelpful inward-looking theology elabo-
rated at the expense of a Pauline theology of the outer
world.

Again, a youthful organism takes risks in stride. It is
certain, sometimes to the point of arrogance, of its own
powers. An aging organism begins to reckon its steps, to be
conscious of the hostilities of its environment, to foresee,
secure, batten down. A youthful mind achieves its maturity through crisis and combat; an aged one hides out
from its world, a threat. An aging body must recoup itself
more often; its energies return to it diminished. But perhaps the most pitiful evidence of an old age that has lost
touch with reality is the way in which the aged tend to
live among the dead. The line between the living and the
dead gradually loses clear demarcation. The enfeebled
old prefer to summon ghosts rather than to confront living
men.

Within systems of authority, this tendency shows itself
in a rigid bias in favor of a rule. Conclusions, adaptations,

the thought and struggle required for living judgment—all these are avoided by a simple tactic: by summoning up the example of founders or dead heroes. In such a way, the law is divorced from life, to the point where any real understanding of the struggles or hopes of living men dissolves. The minds that we speak of no longer respect history as the evidence of Providence—unless that history is a closed one.

The personalism that must govern all life that deserves the name human is beyond the powers of the enfeebled, who tend to become querulous and distrustful of whatever is new or unfamiliar. The condition is worsened when mankind wears a young face, when energy, clumsiness, and a generally unfinished look come before men who regard all differentiation as a threat. To an aging mind, youth is a disease that time will cure. Meantime, read us the law!

The Church can have no part in such an impersonal retreat from life. The word of Christ, living on in His Body, implies that whatever is real, whatever commands attention and releases the energies of living minds, is also reductively personal. From the Holy Trinity to the humblest insensate fragment of creation, the universe is joined, lowest to highest element, in a dense, carefully wrought web of analogy and serviceability. The Incarnation has made this truth both dramatic and immediate; Christ, in becoming man, has taken all things to Himself. Moreover, in saving man, He has in a mysterious way touched inanimate creation with a longing to be enfolded in man's hope. St. Paul could write that all creation groans in travail, awaiting the redemption of the sons of God (Rom. 8:22-23).

Through the cosmic scope of Christ's vocation, His Church includes the richest variety of being. Indeed, all reality finds place in her, according to hierarchy, according to a convergence of all things on man and of all men finally in one Man. The universe of nature and grace, of beauty and anguish, of human hope and nobility, together with the changeful face of the natural world—all stands as the radiant exfoliation of the "perfect manhood" of Christ (Eph. 4:13).

But in all this variety, the person remains the heart of the matter, for Christ as for Christians. Indeed, when men gather to serve His honor in whatever way, He is in their midst, the animating heart of their steadfast will to service and love.

Still, when all the evidence of Scripture has been accepted in principle, it remains true that personalism in the Church will never be easy or automatic. An ideal of life, exalted and exigent at once, does not resolve the difficulties that invariably face men who have experienced a common ideal and have resolved to perpetuate it. In the first fiery days of their resolve, difficulties and conflicts will not be so apparent; but in the nature of things, they are bound to assert themselves. For the law intervenes, whether one would have it so or not; permanence demands at least a minimum rule, and with the advent of law the difficulty of setting a balance between the personal and normative becomes quite formidable.

As time passes, the danger increases that one or another aspect of the rule tends to become autocephalous and that the life of the group turns imperceptibly from its first great vision of Christ and the human family in favor of security and stability. Such a danger is indeed evident and sobering in many religious groups in the Church of today. Dissociation of a pattern of life from the realities that first breathed energy and purpose on the members—dissociation of vows, prayer, and works from the deepest needs of man, and from a sense that the Chruch must serve those needs—this puts our problem in its simplest terms. And one should perhaps add that the difficulties experienced by groups within the Church are evidence of a dissociation painfully present in the Church at large—the separation of sacramental and sacrificial action from its consequences in the community of Christ and in the world.

Yet in contrast to this, the early Church achieved an admirably unified understanding of itself. As the Acts of the Apostles tells in so many subtle ways, the Church contained and explored all the aspects of a true religious life in a vivid and practical unity. She saw herself under the symbols of Spirit and Blood, the Holy Spirit and the Eucharist. But the Blood was not Christ's only, "still warm upon our altars" (Augustine); it was also the blood of Christians, poured out in labor, in the works of mercy, and in martyrdom (Ignatius of Antioch). And the Spirit was not only the gift of Pentecost, once given and withdrawn; it was, more exactly, the Pentecostal event that was the Church herself. The Church was the single and crowning evidence of Spirit in the world. She was the breath of God living in men (Augustine).

And the Savior of men, as she understood well, had despoiled Himself in His Incarnation (Phil. 2:8). He had taken His stand within a mankind essentially impoverished, deprived as it was of the sense of God and of community (Rom. 1:18). And where the Savior led, the Church would follow. Poverty of spirit in the Church, nourished by the Old Testament and the sayings of Jesus, helped the Church mightily in her tasks of saving compassion. Both as sign and reality, spiritual poverty, as she came to understand, was profoundly unitive. As reality, it brought home to her the truth of her mission to the world, her struggle on behalf of human survival and dignity. As sign, poverty opened the eyes of her mind and heart, in-

viting the deepest understanding of the human condition
—the incompleteness of man, the summons of life to self-
donation and heroic charity, the social nature of man's
exodus and return to the Father.

Historically, renunciation of the world as a way to God
appeared in early Christianity most strikingly. It took the
form of monachism. The poor man was both sign and
reality; his self-deprivation was both parabolic and heroically real. His renunciation was a kind of experiment, art-
fully controlled and isolated, of the existence of man as a
center of demonic conflict. The anchorite cleared all debris
and distraction from his life; the enemy even of modified
good, as Anthony and Cassian wrote, he stood in an arena,
a wilderness, in order to confront the powers of darkness
and of light. In the image of the Messianic One, the solitary even invited this combat, by "impelling himself,"
"being violently drawn" into the desert. (Mark's language
in regard to our Lord is quite striking.) In such a way the
early Church prolonged its experience of the suffering
servant, of Him who had come not to be served but to serve.

The reality of man as creature of God was a special insight of the Old Testament. The Savior perfected this
truth in the creation of a new community of sons of God.
But the sons of God lived on in a fallen world. If men
went into the desert, then, it was in faithful submission to
the truths both of sonship and of sin. The burning days,
the fierce deprivations, the solitude were the appropriate
setting for the drama of God's love for man—a drama in-
volving those who were acutely conscious of their inner
poverty and determined to face it out. For as such men
knew, they bore within them the seeds of rebellion; their
sonship of God was damaged. They were also sons of Adam,
conceived in sin and liable to sin.

If Christianity modified this somber picture and gave it

hope, it also bore witness to the profound truth of man's
poverty. Even the holiest of men were of the race of the
anawim. Man's essential poverty, in face of the prevenient
love of the Father, was his inability to enter the kingdom
of Christ. It is instructive in this regard to realize that as
St. Paul's preaching witnesses, Christians understood well
the inner powerlessness even of believing men (Rom.
3:23). And to speak of early liturgical practice, we recall
that almost from the first days of the Church, neophytes
were admitted to the community by way of a dramatic
ceremony of stripping and combat. It was the Church's
way of dramatizing a struggle that was implicit in her
view of life, a drama that life in the Church would only
intensify.

But long before the renunciation of some Christians took
the form of monachism, the Church was aware of the social
consequences of Christ's coming—a coming that brought
Him among us in the form of a servant. The poor, the
defenseless, the maimed were her special honor and joy
because of the special aura Christ had invested them with.
Page after page of the Gospels bear witness of the understanding that Christ was indeed the Messiah announced
by Isaiah. "The Spirit of the Lord is upon me because he
has anointed me; to bring good news to the poor he has
sent me" (Lk. 4:18; cf. Is. 61:1, Mt. 13:54–58, Mk. 6:1–6).
Every poor man was, in fact, the sacrament of the great
Poor Man. It followed, then, that action on behalf of the
poor was a gesture in favor of Christ. "You gave me to
eat . . . you covered me . . . you visited me" (Mt. 25:35–36).
We note the vital, realistic personalism that flourished in
the early community life of the churches. Poverty of spirit
meant that one deprived himself, after the example of
Christ, in order to relieve the poor. In the Christian view
of things, in fact, it worked no benefit to deprive oneself

unless one did so in favor of another. To deliver over one's goods, even one's body, was unavailing when such action was taken in an inhuman vacuum. It was, in effect, an errant vanity, a reversion to stoicism; it profited nothing (I Cor. 13). Christian poverty of spirit, however, stood in great contrast to this subtle egoism; it was in fact the Christian eye and hand, seeing and serving the community of man. Luke gives us our lead in the summary sections of the Acts; the community experience of Christ was renewed at the altar in the breaking of bread; but worship had its natural consequence in the breaking of bread for the hungry, in service and availability, in concord of mind and heart, in communion and community (Act 2:42, 4:32).

Church authority was impregnated with the same spirit; it took its stand on service of the community (Jn. 13: 12–14, Acts *passim*). The credentials of authority were based on a personal choice of men by the Holy Spirit (Acts 13:2, 4). The divine choice was ratified by the Church; the special excellence of authority rested, in consequence, not on distinction and honors but on a fullness of mystical gifts that fitted those in authority for an eminence of service. Peter, Paul, James, and Barnabas thus showed forth the light that had first broken on men in Galilee and Judea, the light of a Lord whose vocation was an unassuming daily gift of Himself on behalf of man's need. Such was the experience of the Church in Jerusalem and, later, in Corinth and the gentile world.

When the Church was expanding into new lands, the reality of spiritual poverty took an extremely practical form. *Koinonia*, the community spirit that had flowered in the Church at Jerusalem, now took on a larger task; the gentile communities, as beneficiaries of the mother church, showed their gratitude and solidarity by a collection "within the household, ecumenical" for the poor of Jerusalem. (2 Cor. 9ff.) Paul was anxious to bring home to the gentile believers the deepest meaning of the collection. He saw no better way than such mutual giving to dramatize within the new communities the self-sacrifice that Christ had undergone and taught: "Being rich, he became poor for your sakes" (2 Cor. 8:9). The collection was not meant to show a painless or juridical or automatic unity. One could not contribute to others as a Christian and remain personally unaffected, Paul implied. Such an illusion would be profoundly untrue to the reality of the Church, whose unity remained a constant struggle, a deprivation of each for the sake of each, a drama of man's incompleteness, which only the flesh and spirit of the neighbor could make whole.

In such a way, the collection bound men of faith more closely to one another, by a cord of mutual awareness and love. Paul records, in this regard, an otherwise unknown saying of Jesus: "It is more blessed to give than to receive" (Acts 20:35). Indeed, in the collection, all men benefit; the superficial differences that mask the truth of existence from human eyes are stripped away. "Here there is not 'Gentile and Jew' . . . 'slave and freeman'" (Col. 3:11). Differences are liquidated; men stand in their essential nakedness before the Father. The Church's experience of Christ and of the community is united.

As the Church came to know and teach by such practical steps, all men, in their deepest existence, are poor men. Only Christ could "become poor"; it remains for mankind to explore and accept a poverty that, from the point of view of God and the neighbor, is simply a datum, a fact— the appalling truth of our state. Men are poor in grace, poor in submission before life, poor in the capacity for love. The poverty of man is mysterious and ironic in its distribution; according to measure, it deprives the pagan and the pharisee of the only riches worth possessing. And its irony consists in this: conditions of life and habits of mind deny to each of these the precise riches he had most counted on —the pagan is denied his humanism, the pharisee his God.

On the other hand, poverty of spirit has its ironic rewards. When realized and accepted, this inner deprivation and sense of deficiency can become an overmastering motive for exploring life in an entirely new way—with humility and compassion. In such a case, man's incompleteness becomes a source of eruptive new life, of artistic, intellectual, and religious energies that over the centuries have, in fact, contributed heavily to the enrichment of man.

The drama of poverty, then, understood in its large sense, opens before men the truth of their existence. The drama deserves to be called both classical and biblical in its power to illuminate the rhythms of life, in its vast implications for all men. It speaks of the meaning of nature and of God, of grace and creation, of life as gift and achievement. It destroys some lives violently, in a storm of covetousness and pride; it invites other lives into quiet, contemplative moments. It opens vast perspectives of human loss and gain, of refusal and acceptance.

To speak more exactly of the religious life, the exploration of poverty of spirit is of great help in understanding a vocation in the Church. To be poor in the evangelical sense is indeed to be involved deeply with God and man; it is to become a protagonist in human life, a drama that, in its deepest meaning, is simply the struggle toward growth, awareness, and love.

Drama is a purifying clash of spiritual forces, a struggle of heroic wills, a struggle which is intensely personal but which still implies immediate and explosive social consequences. In tragic drama, the defeat of the hero is the prelude to his victory, and heroism is an achievement won from the deepest reaches of suffering. At the outcome of the tragedy, man stands renewed in his being, in the acceptance of his identity as son and brother. The hero has won a definition that is both genetic and final. Man's victory over egoism and the forces of evil restores him to the original form willed by God—a form postulated by man's deepest instincts, deformed by sin, and finally restored in Christ. But his new identity also makes him a man of the future, a sign of the last day. It is as son and brother that men will enter into God.

The man of poverty of heart is a protagonist in this essential human drama. In him, the struggle of all men lives on in an intensified form. He is protagonist in a classical sense—a man of unusual or even heroic stature who faces a crucial choice that will decide his future. Up to the moment of crisis, such a man may have been open to life, generous, moral, but he has remained untested by life. He is still burdened with the influences of a past that has been the source of both his potential greatness and his limitations. He has not yet suffered or, indeed, known what it is to stand in the breach, responsible for others, willing to take risks for their sake. But now, by a mysterious summons of God, he enters a particular form of Christian life; he begins, at least remotely, to sense that both God and man stand in his path, that his life is about to fork off in mysterious and unknown directions. And the struggle begins, with all its accompaniment of bewilderment, humiliation, clumsiness. It is a struggle whose outcome he cannot know; but he senses obscurely that his crisis will, in fact, have immeasurable spiritual consequence for himself and for others. The grace of Christ is beyond doubt offered him in an unusual degree, to tide him over; but grace will not come to draw him aside from the struggle or to remove obstacles from his path; rather, grace will heighten and deepen the struggle. It will multiply the occasions of choice, invite his life more deeply into the mainstream of human and sacred history, not like a corpse riding a current, but as seer, creator, and lover.

One of the rewards of such an experience, among many that might be mentioned, is a growing skill at making choices that favor God and men. The practical implications of this skill, in psychology, in spiritual health, and in the apostolate, are almost numberless. Here, one must at least mention the example of men whose lives were unselfish and imaginatively open. One thinks in this regard of the history of Abraham; of the Exodus people; of the example of our Lord, especially in the tradition of Luke; of the early Church communities; of the monachist and monastic reforms; of the renewal worked in the Church by Francis of Assisi and Ignatius; of the modern movements that have drawn their inspiration from Charles de Foucauld and Thérèse of Lisieux. It seems worthy of note that an insistence on poverty of heart is a constant theme whenever the Church is urged to renew herself and to take stock of her resources in view of new needs in society.

Today, consecrated poverty of life in the Church is an extremely variable calling, depending on traditions, on present cultural and enonomic conditions, and on attempts at adaptation in the apostolate. Current efforts at renewal seem to have their most striking example in the Charles de Foucauld movement and the experiments undertaken among the urban destitute. It seems worth noting in passing that the Foucauld groups are undergoing their greatest success in France, precisely at a time when other forms of religious life are experiencing an acute crisis, and when some of them are even threatened with extinction. The strong response to the Foucauld spirit seems to arise from its inner genius; it is a spirit that is both practical and flexible. It undertakes the consecrated life humbly and experimentally at the side of deprived men and women. The life of the members, rigorous as it is, includes an intense interior life. The communities, open, direct in speech and action, affect even unbelievers as a simple, authentic illustration of the gospel pages. The members work for their living, as did St. Paul. Without self-consciousness or primitivism, they live the lives of the destitute in the large cities, adapting to local conditions and needs, whether on docks or in mines, factories, or prisons. They are marked by a kind of inspired fundamentalism of action, avoiding ideologies on principle and, without propaganda or direct social reform, relying on the power of presence and witnessing.

The Foucauld groups are an example of a new beginning. The question of the renewal or restoration of older groups in the Church is, of course, bound to be more complicated. Still, those who attempt renewal can always learn from the fresh starts that are rather numerous today. In the case of the Foucauld groups, one can even recognize a kind of striking modern example of the experience and methods of the older religious orders, whose first members begged and worked for their living, served in hospitals for incurables and the poor, and labored and died among the destitute.

Even a cursory look at Church history will require one to admit that the externals of poverty of religious orders today, especially in the United States, stand in strong contrast to the practices of the same orders some hundred years ago. They have made their cultural adaptation with thoroughness and alacrity. But whether all of them retain their poverty of spirit in a way that is both a viable sign and a reality is a question that responsible men are bound to continue asking.

Religious poverty in American Catholic life in our own time would perhaps invite our attention to the following facts. They are an attempt, admittedly clumsy and extremely general, to bring the fact of world poverty into focus.

If, in imagination, we were to compress the present population of the world, now more than three billion, into a group of a thousand persons living in a single town, the brutal contrasts of affluence and destitution, of comfort and horrifying need, would be vivid indeed. Thus 60 persons would represent the American segment of the town, 940 the bulk of the world population. The 60 Americans would control half the total income of the town; the 940 would share, as best they could, the other half. The 60 Americans would have an average life expectancy of seventy-one years; all others in the town would die, on the average, before forty. The 60 Americans would enjoy fifteen times as much of all material goods as the rest of the townspeople on the average. They would produce 16 percent of the total food supply, would consume 14 percent of it, and would keep most of the remaining 2 percent in storage. The 60 Americans would, moreover, control and use twenty-one times as much petroleum as the others, twelve times as much electric power, twenty-two times as much coal, fifty times as much steel. The lowest-income groups among the 60 Americans would be better off, on the average, than most of the other townspeople. The contrast of wealth and poverty in our world town would widen out in ever-larger areas of misery. Literally, most of the non-Americans would be poor, hungry, sick, and ignorant. Almost half would be unable to read or write.

In the light of all this, it remains quite probable that a renewal of the sense of poverty in the Church will always depend in large measure on the sense of their own life and times that believers have grasped. The age is past—if, indeed, it was ever present—when men could be effectively poor in spirit and remain at a distance from the fate of the majority of men. And when we consider man's fate today, it is clear that it ranges through a very wide spectrum of destitution, from the obvious and degrading kinds in the underdeveloped countries to the less conspicuous but omnipresent poverty of the slums of our great cities. A sense of this universal suffering, of such extent and implication as to beggar description, cannot but color a sense of what the vow of religious poverty is all about; it would bring home to believers the fact that there can be no such thing in the Church as an impersonal or apersonal poverty that would presume to please God.

Moreover, renewal of spirit cannot simply be legislated. Law is chiefly useful to religious men when it recalls them to their genuine tradition. But the law alone, unaccompanied by inner change, will never be effective in the midst of a cultural drift that runs strongly in an opposite direction. And a strong and even fierce drift, that of national and Western affluence, is exactly the situation that poverty of spirit in the Church must take into account today. It is a current in which most clerics, religious, and laymen are, in the nature of things, immersed. The majority of American Catholics grow up in middle-class homes and parishes; if they enter the religious or priestly life, hardly any of them will have had the experience of earning a living. In seminaries and novitiates, moreover, the atmosphere is generally permissive and generous with regard to material things. After ordination or vows, they are generally assigned to apostolates that serve middle-class Catholics. It is not to be thought wonderful that such a world is almost universally mistaken by them for the lot of the majority of men. That they open their eyes and see the real world is perhaps the first thing required of them.

It remains true also that material well-being is always an

ambiguous blessing for the Church. As Barbara Ward has pointed out, the affluent are generally inclined to resist social change with all the force at their command. No personal need presses on them to bring about change; and as long as their lives are stable and comfortable, conditions in society, even when most deplorable, remain for them largely an abstraction. If their hearts remain closed before the sufferings of others, they often see the lot of most men only as a personal threat to their well-being. Conditions today in Latin America, by way of example, show with what fierceness a minority fights against the curtailment of its own privileges, even when such privileges are morally indefensible in view of the ills that afflict the vast majority in the same society.

It is pertinent to reflect that the penalties of affluence touch churchmen too. The effects of this are often seen in the apostolate. Tardiness and hesitation and lack of imagination in meeting the realities of social life, lack of moral insight, arrival on the scene of crisis only when the crisis is past—such failures as these may be at least remotely related to the relatively closed circle in which most churchmen live.

It is also important to realize in this regard that radical renewals of spirit and adaptations of methods do not take place in historic vacuums. So intermingled are the processes of grace and history that the Church cannot, at any period, escape the pressures of history, the questions and doubts and agonies that social upheaval always gives rise to. As the Vatican Council has shown dramatically, modern life has raised painful questions that the Church must face—questions that revolve around man's hopes, his needs, the forms that he longs to see life take. The attempt to face these questions squarely, not necessarily with answers, since for many of them there are no answers, but with sympathy and compassion—this is indeed a sacred responsibility. It is a burden that can also bring new maturity to the Church herself, as every attempt to meet life with honesty and courage invariably does; it can shape the mind of the Church anew to that "mind . . . which was . . . in Christ Jesus" (Phil. 2:5).

Such is the ideal. But it is evident to any realistic observer of Church history that churchmen are not always ideal men. They are human. What is more, they are often fearful, overprudential, and unconvinced that the realities most men must wrestle with and suffer under have any large claim on their attention. And decisions in the Church —the directions and climate of life there—are usually, in the nature of things, in the hands of such men. As a consequence, the Church herself necessarily takes on the features of her sons; she appears safe, tardy in action, unwilling to admit change, unwilling to abandon reliance on material power, prestige, and honor in favor of a more dramatic and fundamental gospel spirit.

But it remains true, and will bear saying once more, that religion justifies its claims upon mature men when it leads them deeply into the experience of God and of mankind. All else is secondary, and the test of the vitality of the Church in any age is precisely her determination to keep secondary things in second place in favor of the gospel and of Him whom it announces. And the gospel insists on our point; the religion of Jesus is worship of the Father "in spirit and in truth" (Jn. 4:23). The religion of the Savior is, at the same time, dedication of His human energies and resources in the service of human need; far from justifying man by the rote of dogma or moral code, the Spirit of Christ penetrates the flesh and spirit of man with a larger understanding, at once disquieting and healing—a sense of the human condition and the need of a response. "As long as you did it for . . . the least of my brethren, you did it for me" (Mt. 25:40).

Modern life is pressing these gospel truths on us at every point. The needy are everywhere; their condition is appallingly evident to all who have eyes to see. Moreover, men who claim no religious faith at all are seeking their own dignity and fulfillment in serving these needs. They are dedicating themselves at the price of personal comfort and security, often leaving their homeland and family, giving of their intellectual and technical resources wherever need is evident. And such service deserves to be called a sacred enterprise; it is grace or, at the very least, a preparation for grace.

Catholics who understand that their world is sacred evidence of God's plan for mankind are also awakening to the crisis. They have accepted the relationship that binds human suffering to the Christ who came "not to be served, but to serve." And the reward of their sacrifice is a double one: they attract the attention of the world to the Church by their gentle apologetic of service, and they become the shapers of man's future.

Indeed, an understanding of the world under its sign of poverty is so important a question that to renew the sense of poverty within the Church is almost equivalent to a renewal of the whole fabric of her life. One can only rejoice that the Vatican Council has taken account of the effect that men of poverty of spirit can have on the world. In the judgment of that world, there is no more powerful witness on behalf of a philosophy of life than the unspoken determination of dedicated men to stand beside the struggling and deprived in their battle toward the light. This is the judgment that current life is promulgating with constancy and persistence; it says simply: help, direct, enlighten, clothe, feed the living, bury the dead, minister to all. And so urgent is the law that summons us that the future of man takes the shape of this cry. Man in possession of the world's riches—material, cultural, spiritual—either will read the text right, serving man in his most difficult hour, or will himself be swamped and destroyed by the gathering fury of man's despair.

2. Marriage

Marriage: A Mystery

THE DIGNITY OF marriage is one with the dignity of human creation. In the beginning, man and woman were created as images of God. Each had the power of knowledge and love; moreover, through the gift of God's communicated life, each had the power to penetrate the other with a divine principle and, through the other, to release the love of God into all creation.

Precisely as man and woman, each possesses qualities that are highly complementary, that find completion in mutual life. And each has the further power, through grace, to remind mankind of the God who has created. "They shall be two in one flesh" (Gen. 2:24). The mysterious call of the flesh is meant to be answered by each, and it is answered in another way by the God who increases His life in them. The flesh is a door through which each enters the spirit of the other to be enlightened and refreshed. Each has become the instrument of God in the search for God.

We are told in the Book of Genesis that God gave man dominion over all creation, to name and use (Gen. 2:19). In the Hebrew sense of the term, to name is to express one's dominative power. All creation is subject to man; man is to recognize it and to make it his own. But he recognizes it as something separate from and beneath his personal dignity.

We note a great contrast to this scene in another, in which man confronts woman for the first time. The scene of dominion, of distinction even, is radically altered here. Woman is not different in any radical sense; she is one with man, sharing with him the power of knowledge and love. So his meeting with her is an immediate act of recognition: "This now is bone of my bones, and flesh of my flesh: she shall be called woman, because she was taken out of man" (Gen. 2:23).

Not only intelligence and the power of love mark woman; in the mysterious depths of her soul, in her destiny, in her power of choice, in her independence, she is one with man. Remaining faithful to God and to each other, man and woman will enjoy the same reward; sinning together, as the account of Genesis goes forward, they pay an identical price. And the beginnings of their life together indicate that the first marriage, although no sacrament, is already holy by the declaration of God Himself. No power on earth could dissolve a contract meant, as history moved forward, to be an image of an even greater reality.

But marriage in the Old Testament had to await its great moment. The sacred nature of the contract was clear from the beginning. Love in the flesh expressed, through the flesh, a thing holy and pleasing before God; it needed only the word of the Savior to make it expressive of the gift of His grace. In the Old Testament, the love of man and woman could also be a vessel of the Divine Life. Could a human contract, the giving over of rights of the body to each other, also confer sanctifying grace on the contracting parties? This, of course, was a question that only God could answer. And He did answer it in Christ, His Son. And the answer was yes (Jn. 1:14). Indeed, without the Incarnation it could never have occurred to men to pose the question of this larger meaning of the contract of marriage.

The question of marriage as a sacrament, as Christ came to announce it, is one of the central questions of reality; it involves what we might call God's whole attitude toward creation. Does He love His creation sufficiently to wish to penetrate it completely, to embrace it in His Person, to give a blessing to all the material universe, not from a distance or through the prophets, but in His own Person? This is St. Paul's great intuition on marriage. He sees it from the point of view of the Incarnation, and from the vantage point of that event he expresses a view of the universe. God's answer to man's hope was a marriage answer: "I do." And "the Word was made flesh, and dwelt among us" (Jn. 1:14).

Our conception in grace, our "new creation," as Paul calls it (Gal. 6:15), depends on God's acceptance of the material world as this world grows conscious in Christ. And the human beginnings of the mystery take place in the body of a woman. The Incarnation was, among other things, a mystery of sex. God sought, in order dramatically to express His view of the world, the consent of a woman. Human flesh was seized upon, as the Fathers of the Church do not hesitate to say, by the action of the Holy Spirit. "The Holy Spirit shall come upon thee" (Lk. 1:35). He came not only upon her soul but also upon her body, to do a work that could be done only in a human body. In such a way the body of Mary became a symbol of what we might call the literalness, the realism of God in proclaiming from within creation that "all the things that he had made . . . were very good" (Gen. 1:31). And this sacred flesh of the Virgin, penetrated and made fruitful by the Holy Spirit, the bearer of the Incarnate Word, was finally assumed into heaven. She was God's sign that what was taken from the earth would one day see His face. So in her, mankind reads its destiny; we are brought forth to heaven by a marriage. This is one of the central symbols of Paul, the marriage of the Word with our nature through the consent of the woman.

This marriage of God with the human family, with man's universe and his history, has, like every true marriage, two great qualities. It is first of all faithful. The Fathers of the Church declared, "What the Word of the Father assumed once, He assumed forever." The Body that rested in Mary's arms, the Body of the altar, the Body of the faithful, is one with the Body seated at the right hand of the Father, perpetually interceding for us, bearing His wounds for our sake, a perpetual evidence to the world of the love of the Father for men. The fidelity of the marriage of the Word with our nature means, in effect, that the event of the Incarnation has never been canceled; what God has sworn, He will not repent (Ps. 110:5).

It was a vow that brought Him to the very depths of the human condition, to poverty and death in the world, to the most anguished and intimate realization of what it was to be man. It brought Him to the heights of the human condition, as Paul and John remind us. It was this sacred humanity that arose, the first fruits of all the dead; for richer for poorer, for better and worse, He is ours. He ascended into heaven and sits at the right hand of the Father.

At the Last Supper His heart was filled with this imminent departure and the eventual reunion; He spoke of the wine that He would "drink . . . new with you in the kingdom of my Father" (Mt. 26:29). The author of the letter to the Hebrews sees Him as the faithful bridegroom who awaits in glory this meeting with His bride, the Church, won at such price. The Church, still journeying far from Him, awaits the day of His return with an indestructible hope.

The second quality of marriage, illuminated by the Incarnation, is its fruitfulness. The main theological evidence is in St. John's writings (Jn. 13–17) and in St. Paul's view of the Church (Eph. 5:24–25). A death and victory within the human condition have brought about the birth of the new humanity. The scope of Paul's vision carries our reflections on marriage forward from Genesis to the Incarnation and then to the Church's reflections on her own nature as set down in Scripture.

We are on firm ground in the conviction that Christian marriage must follow a pattern, a cycle of events laid down for it in the marriage of Christ with man. In this sense, the pattern, the spiritual course of a marriage, is quite clearly written between the lines of the Gospels. Marriage is, in fact, a vocation in Christ.

Baptism introduces us into Christ's life. Thenceforth the Christian biography is clear. A series of divine events is to be encountered in the course of human life and death. It is a pattern first experienced by Christ in His flesh—*passio, resurrectio, ascensio* is the cycle the liturgy speaks of. The Christian is to know a public life, a death, a resurrection, and finally an eternal union with the Father.

Now, according to one's state of life, his talent, and a congeries of important human circumstances, this Christian cycle is fulfilled in quite different ways. Marriage introduces an adult refinement into the baptismal experience. It prompts one to say, in effect, to another person in the Church: "Through you I shall experience my public life, my passion, my death, my resurrection, my ascension." It implies that two destinies are so closely joined that this cycle, this divine process of grace, will be undergone "in one flesh."

Marriage reminds one through another human being of what baptism first declared. There would be no life without a prior death. There will be no death that is not verified on the public scene, and all this "in Christ Jesus." So the sacrament of marriage brings it about that as far as human beings can, in the universe of grace, two persons will win eternity for each other. This is so profoundly true that we cannot hope to approach its profound meaning. We have in no other relationship so powerful an example of the eternal effect one human being can have on another when each has delivered himself to the other and when God intervenes in their mutual gift so that each becomes the vessel of His divine life. "I take you for richer, for poorer" implies "I offer you a grace that will guarantee your continuing to take me until death. Our first embrace, our first act of love, is at the altar, where our hands meet. Through this consent I pour new life into you. This is our first wedding present to each other—grace."

Reflections on the marriage grace necessarily imply a realistic and concrete view of life. The grace of marriage, like the grace of any state of life—the grace of the priesthood, the grace of the single life—does not operate in a vacuum. Neither does it create a dream world or merely extend adolescence into adult life. It does something infinitely more difficult and valuable. It gives to daily life a divine meaning and interior quality, the possibility of merit. In marriage, grace makes of each partner the first hope of the other—for human development, for eternal life. Each, to speak realistically, becomes more able to work with life as it is. The grace of marriage is the very opposite of escapism. It offers the energy to plunge into a most difficult vocation, the energy to seize on the meaning of life, to continue to grow in a human way, and to bear into eternity a wealth of human achievement.

The grace of the sacrament, if it is truly itself and truly expressive of the energies of the risen Christ in mankind, must enable each of the partners to die each day to selfishness and pride and sensuality, to the hardness of nonlove, to the incipient paganism that threatens to make every man a castaway. It is true that within the passion and death cycle of marriage, each partner becomes the executioner of the other. That their life might become itself a life of holiness and growth, a death must be its first act. Without any hint of dramatics or hysteria or pride, each says, in effect, to the other: "I die daily, but through you, and this is my law of life. I accept the daily death implied in a gift that is lasting and faithful. I could not continue to belong to you except by death to myself. A tide of selfishness and impatience and lust would bear me away from you unless I were anchored to your body, unless I clung to you with all my might. You are the cross to which alone I am attached." So each becomes for the other the *crux fidelis* the faithful cross that will be the eventual glory of the other.

The grace of the marriage vows works this adhesion, body and soul—an adhesion to life as it is. Each partner declares to the other his radical incompleteness, both in nature and of grace. It is on such a stage, human, mysterious, and exigent, that the vows bring forth their fruit.

We are continually led back by way of the truth of marriage to the truth of the Incarnation. When God became man, He was not staging a play or a farce; the Incarnation was the entrance of God into history, into a family, into home and workshop, into rejection or acceptance by human beings. The graces of the Word Incarnate flowered in an entirely human framework of life.

And so with marriage. Its graces affect the structure and quality of life itself; they confer the wisdom to accept life and its unmeasured mystery, to confront clear-sightedly everything blatant and hackneyed and secondary, to restore and heal. So St. Paul's idea expands like the expansion of the heart; his thought moves from symbols to the reality and back again. He begins by speaking of the Incarnation, leads on to marriage, thence to the Church, and often his thought ambiguously ranges around these three. And his consummate insight is that the symbol of the perennial love between Christ and His Church is Christian marriage. The continuing acceptance of life, of each other, dramatizes the divine will to pitch His tent among us, to save man by being present to man, to show His transcendence by a holy immanence. The mutual surrender within marriage declares by implication that God is neither stoic nor Olympian. In the Incarnation of His Son, God declares His will to share the riches of the Trinity, to save by presence and indwelling.

So we have resonances within marriage that are trinitarian, ecclesiastical, and incarnational. Just as man and woman long for warmth and passion, long to express a love that is the very opposite of academic or abstract, so their marriage reminds us of God's impatience with the juridical, the superficial, the extrinsic to life. His pact with us, as He declared, was a marriage. He appeared among us from within one of us, the fruit of a human womb, "what we have seen with our eyes, what . . . our hands have handled" (1 Jn. 1:1). And this holy self-giving continues in the Church through marriage. So Paul's throught flows naturally from the sacrament of marriage to the holy mystery by which Christ wedded Himself to mankind.

Marriage, then, is a historical event that, from the earliest days of history, has been constantly unfolding; its full realization was reached in Christ Jesus, in His Incarnation, in His Church.

Perhaps now we can draw closer to the reality of marriage as it expresses itself in our own times.

Paul, Luke, and John, who describe the sensibility of the early Church with great insight, were convinced of the underlying unity of all vocations within the Church. All men are one in the divine life that opens before all. Unity in Christ explains why vocations, to the priesthood or to marriage, may seem to have great variety and richness in their expression and yet are rooted in the same grace of Christ, poured out on all men. The single gift of Christ explains also why, even though symptoms of failure within vocations may seem to differ, in reality the failures proceed in every case from a like denial of life.

In the priesthood we have cause to mourn how sometimes the priestly mind and heart become sterile. In marriage we note how unity can become a kind of marital coziness, an emotional egoism, a narrowing down of the horizons of early youth. In both cases it is clear that Christians have refused Christic life in its larger potential. A kind of lesser and visible reality has won out over a greater and invisible one; the appearances of life have succeeded in dictating the terms of life. Perhaps we are at a point of understanding with more compassion and insight why the Church claims many good priests but not so many great ones—just as we are a little closer to understanding why there are so many good Catholic marriages and so few great ones. The failure has at least something to do with openness to life or, on the other hand, with hatred of life or fear of life or neutrality toward life.

Marriage as Social Reality

Let us speak finally of the public implications of Christian marriage from the point of view of two great men, one of them a saint of the early Church, one a man of our own times.

The thought of Paul explores two great qualities of Christian marriage. First, this reality, he implies, is *organic*. There is no need to cover once more the ground of his recurrent image of the Church as the Body of Christ (Eph. 1:22–23, 5:29–30; Col. 1:24). The image is, in fact, part of the substance of the modern Church's self-understanding. It is instructive, though, to recall that Paul's impatience with dead or mechanical images reflects a view of life that is searching, unfinished, and crisis-minded. The Body of Christ, of which the Apostle writes with such passion, is a reality of human history. It is subject to time and to human use. It is available before mankind. It wears the clothing of life. It knows what we might call the innocence and pain of a given moment when its own judgments are still as unfinished as a child's. This Body of Christ has a kind of piety toward experience. It has a native instinct for human love, and it loves now well and now badly, now clumsily and now with skill. This Body is holy and it sins; it sins and it repents.

The divine gifts in which it rejoices give it an obscure thirst for God and a piercing thirst for human life. At its best, according to Paul, this Body finds itself ironically present to the pulse and direction of human life, present to the truth that redemption has changed everything and changed nothing. It has changed everything in offering human destiny a new possibility; it has changed nothing until man has freely accepted God for his portion.

And this Body has a strong, exact sense of its own identity; it knows who it is; it is the possession of Christ and of mankind. Its consciousness moves forward in the senses and in darkness. It lives in mystery and it lives in evidence. It stands under divine judgment and it exercises human judgment. And all these simultaneous ironies and apparent oppositions enrich and deepen the community's consciousness and in a particularly acute way make the Church a mediator of human life.

Paul's passionate sense of the reality of the Church assured him that the Body of Christ could not be disembodied. It must be present to the body of man, and it cannot be present there as a neutral or a judge or a tourist or a parasite—it is present as a lover and a friend. Paul's view would certainly imply that only a pagan regression could persuade the Body of Christ that it could deny human life—all its brutality, its mire, and its anguish—without at the same time amputating its own limbs.

This understanding that the Church is a living organism was the source of the practical judgment that Paul was able to bring to bear on events. His sense of the Church was not a false sense of eternity; rather, it was a sense that was exploratory of time and human life. We note throughout his letters to the early Church how human events served to stimulate his adulthood. Crisis found him ready, not with abstraction in place of acts of the will, not with pieties in place of action, not with perpetual tardiness or a paper Christianity, but with a response that was unfailingly courageous and virile and timely.

Secondly, Paul's view of life is *unitive.* In discussing the Church, he relies heavily on Old Testament marriage symbolism, which he sees as a source of intuition from which the mystery of the Church can be clarified. Life in Christ is a marriage. God has declared it so in His Son. In an act that was creative of a new humanity, He embraced mankind as His bride. And that embrace had its implications wherever man would turn. Heaven and earth now stood in friendship. Man was wedded without and within—to his neighbor, to himself, to his own mind and flesh. Man could accept others because he had accepted himself. But Paul sees this wedding image as a reproof also. It reproves the disruptive and hateful tendencies of divorce, the frightful inner rupture so powerfully symbolized in Genesis after the Fall, a rupture that lives on in us. Through this instinct, man arms himself against love—against God, rebellion; against his brother, the will to murder. A history of human hatred and war and fratricide, of opposition to the demands of love is so deeply compounded in man by his inherited sin that every Christian has for his main and lifelong task the attainment of so simple a thing as the love of one brother.

A few reflections of Charles Péguy may also be of point to the present discussion. Christian spirituality, in Péguy's language, is named *mystique*; he translates the word as "the Christian operation, the Christian tactic." In the first version of *Cléo*, he says: "Originally and primitively the mystical life, the Christian operation, consisted not in avoiding the world, but in saving the world; not in fleeing from the times, in separating and cutting oneself off and hiding from the times, but on the contrary, it consisted in nourishing the times mystically through action." Alexander Dru, in his study of Péguy, comments: "The mystical life, that is to say the supernatural life of faith, hope, and charity, is seen by Péguy as a Christian operation. It is the mission of Christianity in this world, so that Péguy's contemplation leads directly into action; and the fulcrum preserving the balance between the life of man in God and the life of man in this world is charity."

The attack that Péguy made on the Catholicism of his day was the immediate result of his discovery of the roots of Christian life. If the mission of Christianity in its Catholic form was to be carried out, the first requirement was a clear view of the times, of the modern world, and an analysis of the future of Christianity. Péguy says, in this regard, "We must not withdraw from the living world in order to contemplate a mystical city. It seems to me that humanity at the present time needs the whole care of all men."

After 1908 the source of all his work was his prayer, so that he could hardly distinguish, in his inspiration, between genius and grace. His contemplation flowed into action. This he translated by insisting that "man's public action must be nourished by his life of grace." He related these two, action and grace, by saying that "they formed a living Christianity, a religion of temporal salvation; this Christianity which is also the religion of eternal salvation." His purpose, as he often affirmed, was to understand the Christian operation not in the abstract but in the concrete situation of man's life, in which man discovers himself.

To speak more nearly of marriage, Pius XI stressed the role of the sacrament both as self-perfecting and as the perfecting principle of society. But it is almost exclusively on the first of these ideas—marriage as a self-perfecting reality —that modern Catholic marriage movements and marriage spirituality have concentrated. By the same token, the second social aspect—marriage as perfective of society—has been largely neglected. The proof of this neglect one finds in the tentative nature of the ventures made by married Catholics in the social arena, as well as in the magnitude of the tasks that they have shied away from. The result of this unwillingness to bear the sacramental energies into public life is a great imbalance in the marriage sensibility itself. Catholic couples are armed to the teeth with prayer and the sacraments, but they find themselves largely bewildered before the chaos of fermenting hope and despair in the world at large.

Marriage spirituality should aim to restore some balance here. It is time to begin exploring and experimenting with the social dynamism of the sacrament of marriage. The dismal and rather childish record of so many Christian couples' groups makes the proposal an expedient one. In social action, Catholics tend to miss large issues; in their training techniques, they tend to substitute a short-circuit enthusiasm for the dolorous long-term spiritual formation that alone will create a lay elite. Hence we have false starts and adolescent frictions, a general lack of freedom and heroism and sense of the essential.

Catholic marriage movements are, in fact, at the present time living off the capital of the pioneer laymen and priests who forged the tools of the movements with a large measure of genius, practicality, and insight. The supposition of the latter was that sacramental fervor, interior formation, gospel and social discussions would lead men and women on to the main event, which they uniformly agreed was the social drama of man, the crisis of justice and poverty throughout the world. But most of the groups today are still "in formation." They are essentially ingroups, strongly oriented to family welfare, evoking no friction, asking no painful or public questions. They have added no significant element to modern public life—whether national or international.

In such a situation, where the formative possibilities of direct, mature action are so largely ignored, it is probably useless to speak of a theory of the spirituality of marriage. After a certain time has elapsed, adult spirituality dies unless it is carried forward into pertinent action; if theories are developed apart from action, they become increasingly academic and unreal.

And considering the lay apostolate in its modern development, there are by now many volumes of theorizing and much tapping and X-raying and diagnosing of the past. Some sort of stalemate has occurred. The Catholic groups sometimes seem to be talking more and more about less and less.

A functional weariness afflicts priests and couples alike. Almost everyone senses it; hardly anyone at all speaks of it publicly. And what is the nature of this weariness among the young and the good, among the formerly hopeful and convinced? It is, at least possibly, a strong symptom that the end of one period of things has come. Catholic marriage groups are at the end of one organic stage and are being invited by the process of growth itself into another. The first stage is consolidated and achieved; it can be kept alive only by the kind of artificial respiration that goes on in so many of the local groups. But what is the new state of things that the married are now invited to enter?

Perhaps in searching for the answer to this perplexing question, an organic simile might be of use. Biologists tell us that in the development of the human fetus, certain physical organs that belong properly to lower organisms appear for a time. These organs assert themselves, exercise their brief, genuine function, and then quickly become residual in favor of further, properly human development. As the months pass, it is apparent that a vital inner form is slowly drawing the whole organism forward into human life, so that at term the infant is equipped to be ejected into life.

Three points emerge here as relative to our topic. First, no organism can achieve itself except by organic stages. Secondly, the final life form of the organism rules over the whole development, so that many characteristics that appear at certain points to be permanent must yield before the good of the being itself. Thirdly, the criterion of what is permanent and what is merely transient in a living being cannot be understood merely in the light of the well-being of individual organs; the criterion is what we might call the life needs of the organism itself. For instance, only the shape of the organism, the life form, can sense whether an arm is more important than a gill; yet at stages each appears, each seriously functions. And yet the one is residual, the other functional and integral to the life of the organism.

By a kind of biology of spirit that is dear to St. Paul, it becomes clear that any organic grouping within the Church undergoes a kind of analagous community gestation. No group comes to maturity except by first undergoing certain stages of life. Men and women bound by a common sacramental bond, a certain community of ideal, a certain vision of life must meet and send out invisible resonances of sympathy and communion and action, slowly and mysteriously setting the structure of a new organism. Nothing else can be done until this is done. But a time is reached when what we might call the primitive group embryology is finished with and the group must ready itself for adulthood.

As an adult organism, the grouping is to be self-sufficient, self-reproductive, and self-conscious. Instead of being merely self-exploratory, it is to become exploratory of its world. Everything about it that was personal and familial must be ready to enter a wider field of action. The group is now equipped to react not merely to the sensuous and the singular and the *quid pro quo* but to the spiritual view, to the wish to know its world. And this is, after all, the first task of an adult—a skill at entering relationships with other adults—relationships of love, thought, and communal action, relationships that will shape life for the individual and the group, that will be formative of history for the community.

Within a group that is truly adult, men and women are

the victims neither of past images nor of parental or pleas-
urable images. Their life is decisive and personalized.
Perhaps the most important thing finally to be said about
such a group is that it does not make the absurd, childish
demand that reality come down to its size. Rather, it
speaks the language of adulthood; it asks only to touch
things as they are, to affect them as they are.

To come again to Catholic marriage groups, it seems
apparent from a hundred signs that the organism is being
urged forward into its world. Everything in the biology of
the spirit, everything in the contemporary world tells us
so. Everything in the frustrations of individual adult Catholics tells us so. The organism must choose its future now.
There is no muscular spasm to eject it into adulthood.
There is only a choice; and that choice, as Christianity
makes clear, is a simultaneous welcome extended to God
and to the community.

When adults refuse God and their world, they do not
merely stand where they stood before the choice and its
consequences became clear. Adults do not remain unchanged by selfishness. The refusal of reality is a massive
return of an adult to the infantile stage of life, the stage
that appears under the image of the maternal womb, an
envelope of safety, peace, helplessness, and passivity.

Are our marriage groups refusing their future and living on in the womb of arrested development? Only they
can answer the question, with the coming of reflective-
ness, courage, and the longing to know their world. One
may perhaps venture, in this regard, to suggest a few areas
of needful action that have been largely neglected by our
Catholic marriage apostolate.

It is clear, first of all, that Christian spirituality has always arisen out of the passion of believers to know and
love the real world—however painful, exigent, and hope-

less life situations may be—out of the passion to act in behalf of man. Spirituality is the Christian response to the risks of life; toward them, believing men bring the practical judgments formed from the Gospels and the altruism awakened at the altar.

An area from which Catholics have generally abstained is that of direct presence and action on behalf of the developing nations. Catholics, out of their available, well-formed communities, are sending only a very few couples abroad. This is a fact, and it must meet the dogmatic truth that both sacramental dynamism and the genius of Catholic Action are designed to produce men and women of great personal freedom and of large personal and social horizons. Against the dogmatic evidence, we find both in the marriage groups and in their chaplains a business-as-usual mentality, while the world takes shape or misshape without them.

The general Catholic failure in the social arena brings us to a further point. It is that of the quality of our formation for Catholic Action. The American Church has, in fact, been operating, since the first developments in lay spirituality some twenty-five years ago, without any large-scale or realistic policy for the formation of lay people. Yet given once more the dogmatic evidence, it remains true that the Church must be as serious in her policies of lay formation as in the formation of her priests. To guarantee the largest response to the will of Christ for mankind, every Christian who offers himself for serious work in the Church should undergo a careful formation in efficiency, fidelity, and intellectual life. The Church has, in fact, accepted this principle as applying to her formation of priests since the Council of Trent.

By way of contrast, we note how the Church rather hopefully drifts along, welcoming the laymen who offer themselves either without any formation at all or with such formation as comes through their own initiative or the efforts of an exceptional priest. But she has no national policy, no assigned resources, no long- or short-term planning in these areas.

In sum, a strong historic sense of Christ's will, as Paul assures us, was the great aid of the Church as she moved into her overwhelming task. Such a sense of things is also available to Christians today, by the assurance of Christ Himself. It would lead believers realistically and courageously into their own times, forbidding them a cowardly love of the past, an unmortified, unrelated spiritual life, egoistic and secure forms of living. In contrast with all such infantilism, a vital sense of the times sees the life of action, the life of man involved in social ferment as the natural flowering of the grace of Christ.

3. The Eternal Youth of the Church

CONTEMPORARY LIFE OFFERS evidence that mankind is entering a new age. The evidence in sum indicates a break with many aspects of man's past—a rupture so unprecedented and abrupt that men are generally at a loss to give it a name, much less to achieve a synthesis of its features. Ours is a period that is intellectually youthful, resourceful and determined in the use of the power at its command. Correctly or not, it is proud of knowing itself and its world and of its ability to use this knowledge to maximum human advantage.

It is an age in which man's knowledge of his universe gathers momentum at headlong speed, in which some aspects of knowledge show a brilliant advance and others lag behind. It is an age of moral and spiritual greatness and of moral and spiritual deprivation; it is admissive of both good and evil in every order, to a degree and kind unimaginable a century ago.

An analogy drawn from youth may be of help here in our reflections on the name and nature of the new age of man. Most grown men have already experienced what psychology tells us: that youth is a period of great turmoil. Youth does not easily or painlessly integrate its powers; it takes hold strongly of one phase of history or one aspect of the world and concludes that it is in touch with things as they are. During his youth, man is not yet fully equipped to move forward into his world. Rather, the hands of man or the heart of man or the passions of man move forward with a certain clumsy assertive autonomy. But man as man is not yet fully able for his task.

Again, youth takes hold of one truth and thinks it has grasped the body of truth; even when it has come to some sense of objective values, it remains unaware that much time and effort must be expended before a new idea works its way deeply into life. Fits and starts in knowledge, love, and the use of life are the common experience of youth; youth is hopeful and despairing at once, vehement and insecure, given to wasteful dreaming and sudden eruptive action.

But the period of youth, in an individual or in mankind, is one that must be regarded as crucial. Literally everything depends on youth. By its hands, the future will be shaped or deformed. Human wisdom and truth will find its lodging, if anywhere, in the mind of the young. The accumulated riches of man's spirit will be judged, welcomed, or cast aside by them; youth is, in fact, a seedbed of new choices for or against man.

This, we are told, is a time when the patterns of childish selfishness tend to disintegrate with the growth of a new sense of community. And among the hopeful signs that mankind itself may be coming into adulthood, one notes today a more general and accepted awareness of the community of man. Man is advancing out of a merely personal consciousness, one that is neutral and ignorant of mankind in general. To speak of Western man, events have forced him to revise his guardianship over the destinies of the less advanced people. He is ready, at least, to look on others as equal partners in a communal worldwide venture, in which peace and equity will depend more and more on the efforts of all nations.

This awakening of a universal sense within men implies

a new will—the will to be responsible before an awakened world that judges and condemns those who stand apart from man. When one has become a man, he realizes that man is in mankind. So he must be ready to join hands with the fate of all men, to take responsibility for the good estate of other lives, for the things that all men love and hope for and are working toward.

An enormously significant transition thus opens up before the moral life of mankind. Man is offered the choice of accepting his emerging shape as history's pressures are forming it. But one would be very blind or very foolish to claim that this acceptance of a new world order is as yet unqualified or final. While everything in human life points to the crucial need of rational, peaceful decisions representing the voice of mankind, the pressures against such choices tend to multiply. World technology has opened a Pandora's box of hope, fear, and ambition before the gaze of all. Throughout East and West, a voracious appetite for freedom and power is in the air. The appetite is so consuming that it will not be put off with a dole or a handout or a promise.

This issue, given the new world developments, can be put in extremely simple terms. Is man's future to be constructed of two worlds, of two mankinds, hermetically sealed one against the other—one composed of the free, the affluent, the technologically advanced; the other a Huxleian nightmare of the enslaved, the deprived, and the primitive? No. The decree of the future is written large in every language. The decree says that mankind is one, that all men will be free or all will be slaves, that the whole of mankind will achieve its peace or the race will die in a single conflagration.

So a moral question arises to haunt men who see the direction life is taking but who are stunned and bewil-

dered as they search for means to control the new forces
at man's disposal. In what is man to put his hopes? This is
the great question. Is he perhaps to place his hopes in the
genius of man and the limitless exploitation of the power
of his mind? Many speak and write as though the training
of human minds were the answer to every impasse. They
speak as though reason were the great tool, and a perfect
reason the perfect tool, in the search for a human future.
But the majority of men, sobered by a sense of history, are
certain that the hope as stated is groundless, or nearly so,
without a profound change in the structure of the thought
of modern man. The critics of such a theory concede and
praise the technological brilliance of the new man, filled
with a dynamic and determined curiosity with regard to
the mysteries of nature. But the critique would emphasize a point made as long ago as Plato: that the absence
of a moral sense inevitably makes of man's intelligence the
enemy of man. And man today, it must be admitted, is
generally deprived of a lucid conscience. He is ignorant
even of its central importance to his makeup. So he cannot judge the good of man in relation to the good which
the past shows him or which God reveals in His gospel and
His Church. Deprived of moral enlightenment, modern
man cannot answer with any measure of certainty the
questions life itself has always asked. Who is man? What
is his destiny? And what is the meaning of the forces
which modern life is precipitating and which are shaking
the ground beneath his feet?

Another philosophy of man would suggest that human
hope is to be placed in mankind itself. Each generation of
mankind, the ethical humanists teach, summons new resources to meet the gathering wave; conscience, hope,
capacity for suffering and achievement are the sum of past
ages and the form of the new humanity, a form at once

obscure and irresistible. Every generation adds its gain to what went before; thus the forward movement demonstrates that an inner shape is slowly being revealed, a mounting will to justice and peace and order.

The theory, hopeful as it is, is, in fact, very nearly useless. A theory that represents mankind as indefinitely progressing in conscience and moral insight must immediately strike against the realities of modern life. And those realities show the profound ignorance and emptiness which govern modern lives and which reduce so sharply man's potential contribution to any human future at all. Indeed, the theory speaks of mankind as though the word "mankind" has some occult meaning apart from the actual forms that life is assuming today. It speaks as though actual men and the values they accept or refuse here and now are not the first and, indeed, the only relevant facts; it assumes that some Platonic race of men is waiting just beyond the present crisis to spring from the brow of the gods into the human breach.

But no such genetic miracle can realistically be looked for. A thoughtful glance at today's world would show that more men are living their lives at a minimal level of human meaning. And this remains as true of the affluent societies as of the underprivileged ones. Destitute societies look enviously to the world of material abundance that the developed nations are in process of creating and protecting. And the condition of the affluent societies is at least equally sad. There, human faith and hope are placed squarely in this world; men literally look to nothing beyond time; and within their time capsule, comfort seeking, gadgetry, suburban childishness, and the cult of the senses sharply reduce their potential for knowing and acting upon a real world.

The condition of modern man has been described recently by a Protestant writer in *Presbyterian Theology Today:*

> The fact is not just that Christian assumptions are being questioned by the modern secular mode, but that all religions are questioned and even all attempts to give meaning to reality as a whole and to man's destiny within it.

In sum, the "humanity" goal of the social scientists and the ethical humanists ignores the appalling moral vacuum, the material inequity, and the profound envious unrest that mark the true condition of modern society.

But still another theory is proposed. It would place the hopes of men in the new technology. Man's skills have already shown, in an altogether astonishing way, a mystery of nature and its processes. So it would seem logical that a continuing all-out effort of the best minds would bring about a complete control of the universal energies of our world and a consequent harmony both within man and within his social groupings. According to this view of the world, mankind cannot enjoy inner security or peace while his universe remains in revolt against him or conceals natural forces of which he is not yet master.

The theory must be examined courageously in the light of recent history and of the new discoveries themselves as these are illumined by a philosophy of man. In such a light, it becomes clear that man cannot seriously admit to a goal that, for all its apparent greatness, is strictly instrumental to his person. At best, that is, technology can only serve. But to view technology as a goal of human life is to leave man exposed, as Thomas Merton has said, to a horrifying spiritual inertia on the one hand and to a demonic activism of self-interest, comfort seeking, and conscience-less wealth on the other.

Pius XII has spoken bluntly of this theory and of what becomes of man when he places his hopes in skills and technology to such a point that his spiritual nature is, in effect, violated. Technology becomes capable, Pope Pius has said, of creating "a monstrous masterpiece of transforming man into a giant of the physical world at the expense of his spirit, which is reduced to that of a pygmy in the supernatural and eternal world" (Christmas Message, 1953).

But let us be quite sure of one thing. The current philosophy that places the hopes of mankind in technological advances is something more than a paper theory. It is a theory that is almost universally in command of human life today. The theory is accepted widely throughout the power blocs of both East and West. It is accepted to such a point that it has evolved its own language, modes of thought, and value systems and is powerfully advanced by every means known to modern communication.

The more, in fact, that we of the West encounter the Russians in full day, the more evidently clear it becomes that technology is the hope of man, East and West. Indeed, the categories of East and West tend more and more to lose their usefulness when one reflects on the evidence of common goals, common hope, and common vocabulary governing both blocs. Eastern and Western men are becoming more and more certainly one single man. The new Russian and the new American tend toward moral judgments that often coincide and are governed by a like world view.

Such a statement does not aim to ignore very real differences between the two systems. One is not denying that the Western sense of humanity is generally acute and that in comparison with the Russian it would bear a more rigorous scrutiny. It is clear that we have no will to subjugate or exterminate whole peoples and have never in our history done so. It is clear also that we retain at least to some degree that sense of man and of God that has marked the history of Western man. But even this concession is in need of careful analysis. The moral attitudes of the West are, in fact, growing progressively less reasoned, less commonly assumed, and more sentimental. We are a benevolent people without knowing quite why. Social altruism seems to suit our character and is identified widely with us, but neither we nor our critics think commonly or realistically of explaining our compassion and generosity as being governed by religious conviction. Our mercy toward enemies, our hatred of violence, our energetic respect for good works—these are less and less consciously connected with religious belief. Today, they are generally studied and explained in terms of ethos, sentimental humanism, or world expediency.

So as time passes, our historic spirit, once consciously joined to a belief in God, lies more and more at the mercy of events. We are more easily manipulated by political and military crises. We find it increasingly difficult to bring Christian judgments to bear on the great questions that life is thrusting at us. It grows almost impossible for us to show an inner coherence and consistency in our actions.

And when we face the East, we meet our own image in a way that events are clarifying. The great Russian power bloc, status-conscious, power-minded, massively opposed to God and to man, confronts us across the fear and dread of the rest of the world. A new Russian has emerged. He is urbane and scientifically skilled; he knows the jargon of the new times, a vocabulary that we of the West recognize to our discomfiture as very nearly our own language, reflecting our fears, our values, and, above all, our moral vacillation and doubt.

In spite of everything we pretend to say, East-West

jargon makes our real desires embarrassingly clear. The majority on both sides want comfort, security, white supremacy, undisturbed possession of our wealth. We want these things no matter what the misery of others may be. If human misery is to be relieved, our charity must in no serious way interfere with our own material hopes, the goals we have set for our national well-being.

We are likewise unprepared for domestic social crises. Negroes and Spanish-speaking peoples are largely treated as pariahs. And, intellectually speaking, our situation is not particularly heartening. Our great public universities speak of search, openness to life, and respect for the life of the mind; but they hardly ever give evidence of philosophical conviction of the nature of good, of the existence of God, or of a moral law applicable to the life of man or to his social institutions. Indeed, current evidence suggests that the Christian vision of man, once accepted as the moral underpinning of Western society, has been largely and with a certain finality set aside.

On what then does the hope of modern man rest, once he has put aside the pious clichés that only obfuscate the issues of his true hope? His hope rests on the assumption that a technology, cut off in principle from a Christian philosophy of man, will act as creator and redeemer of a human future. And this hope persists and is subject to serious analysis everywhere in spite of paranoic thinking and fears, in spite of mutual ignorance and emotional irresponsibility in both East and West.

It is the suggested theme of this discussion, then, that the inner life of man today is converging on a single worldwide secular hope. This hope is governed by a disciplined doubt with regard to all religious questions. From it, the religious vision of the world that formerly governed our civilization is on principle excluded.

Now it is clear that in the West at least, so ambiguous a

solution to world fear and despair is inducing a massive crisis in man's spirit. The West, cut free from its Christian past, is involved in a frightful inner struggle, a kind of death agony of the spirit. A complex of shocking ironies tortures its body and soul, dividing flesh from spirit, culture from technology, individuals from societies, time from a sense of eternity.

Exhausted by this inner struggle, men are afflicted with lassitude and inertia in face of the fearful worldwide crises that confront them. Their inner agonies leave them little energy with which to meet the problems thrusting forward from all sides—problems that demand solution as the price of survival. One has only to think of the divisions of the Churches, the universal struggle against ethnic integration, the condition of workers and migrant peoples, automation, the international questions of weapons control, the population rise, material inequities, and the fact that so few can summon the resources of detachment, imagination, and courage needed to meet and to make history.

Man, deprived as he is of self-understanding, weakened in moral insight and courage, has seized on the new scientific spirit as the tool of his hope. And the new sense of technological power offers a present danger to men whose weakened moral sense makes them particularly unready to deal with large moral issues. Sick men cannot summon energy to deal with their world. They may perhaps even fretfully write off a world for which they feel only nausea, contempt, and disillusion.

The shadows lengthen; atomic technology, as Hiroshima and Nagasaki have taught the world, is no respecter of man's greatness or of man's history or of man's achievement. The new technology is amoral; its ironic judgment weighs men in the scales of national interest and military expediency. The ignorant Egyptian fellahin, remote tribal

Nigerians, the intellectuals and artists and technicians of Europe and America, the states of the East—none is safe; and the criteria of human worth—man's greatness, his contribution to his society—no longer apply. They will not save him in the hour when a few men decide whether man shall survive.

Systems of law and order, artistic and scientific achievements, moral conscience, communities and their traditions, the stages of man's struggle toward the light—all are threatened, all are in the balance. In a final crushing irony, it is entirely possible that destruction may come at an hour when man is at last in sight of his goal, when his struggle against poverty, ignorance, and fear may finally have a triumphant outcome.

It is in such a world atmosphere that one must reflect on the Church, on her energies, on her will to be the matrix of man's conscience as he turns to his future. Faced with the new period of mankind—capricious, violent, agonized as it is—we consider the eternal youth of the Church. In so doing, we are exercising the self-understanding that is the Church's perennial skill, implying at once a historic insight and a rare courage.

The self-awareness of which we speak is indeed particular to youth, in its passion for understanding, its suppleness and strength. Such awareness is a skill through which the Church is enabled to judge herself and her world, to see herself as necessarily relative to man, and to move more surely and speedily upon the course of her mandate.

It is clear, by way of beginning, that the youth of the Church is the very youthfulness of Christ. The equation is exact; the Church is one with Him and forms in Him the "one new man," the "perfect manhood" of which St. Paul speaks (Eph. 2:15, 4:13). She was "brought to perfection" in Christ's death and victory; she is the fullness of history, the genetic climax and triumph of all processes, whether of the flesh or of the intelligence or of the spirit (Col. 1:17–20).

This youthfulness frees the Church from the death processes common to the pagan world and to merely human institutions. Reborn in Christ, the Church is impregnated with the life of the Risen One; freed from the stigmata of death and sin, she undertakes to continue in her sacraments and her apostolate a vocation to the Father and to mankind. In this way, she is destined finally to see the Holy One face to face, "one Christ, loving Himself" (St. Augustine).

It must be insisted that the youth of the Church makes her responsible not only to the Father but to mankind also. She is a community of living men within mankind; her youthfulness is purified of all that is capricious or cowardly, evasive in responsibility or childish in ambition. Her youthfulness is faithful to human life, grounded and rooted in love. Love for man and a long experience of mankind have fashioned for her the body of a youth, a body of struggle and search and process, humbly sustained and renewed in its will to holiness, to service, to unfeigned love.

In its deepest mystery, the youthfulness of the Church is the youthfulness of the risen Christ, outpoured on the body of mankind. The energies of the Victorious One have made of the Church a new creation, the image and initial movement of that universal rebirth that His return will bring to pass.

We do well to insist on the biblical thought that lies at the heart of these reflections. It is clearly a matter of God's promise that the Church will never be subject to the processes that decree that all things shall be born, shall have their day, and shall decline.

Unique among all who live, the Church will never die. "I am with you all days" (Mt. 28:20). But this youthfulness is not an intersection of eternity and time, a mere point of contact with no further penetration of this world. In such a case, the Church would have no human features, and believers could in good conscience live on in her at the price of living outside mankind. But such can never be the case. The reality of the Church implies, rather, a penetration of time by eternity; it implies a relationship to God and to human history, a very special way of being in the world, an urgency to be present, to be available, to make a difference in the life of man.

And this relevance comes about, in fact, because the body of mankind supplies Christ with His Body, which is the Church. "You are the body of Christ" (1 Cor. 12:27). In this truth lies a counterbalance to the tendency of equating the Church as mystery with the Church as abstraction or of pleading the transcendence of the Church as a way of avoiding the practical consequences of her immanence. The Church is in the world, as one of her early apologists has said, as the soul is in the body. She grows by the accretion to her being of real men, of the thought of man, of the particular coloration and form implied in culture, in work, in talent, in family ties, in human love, in books and schooling. Moreover, in many important respects the mind of the Church continues to be shaped by the minds of those who come to her, by the expectations of mature men who look clearly at all of life and judge it and who, when they approach the Church or when they live on in her, cannot be presumed to suspend such judgments.

It follows, then, that a love of human life in all its aspects is a substantial of the youthfulness of the Church. Such a statement is not meant to plead a superior kind of humanism as the Church's mission. The conferring of divine life on mankind, it is clear, is the first work given the Church by Christ. She makes of man a "new creature" (2 Cor. 5:17). Man enters through her portals into "newness of life" (1 Jn. 5:12). A new man (Col. 3:1), he is marked by a new name (Apoc. 2:17), and his existence from the time of his baptism forward is the sign within mankind of the "new earth" (2 Pet. 3:13) of the Savior's final victory. And this youthfulness is the substance of Christ's liturgical gift to mankind. The gift forms man to the image of the eternal and victorious Christ; here and now it seals him in the company of the victorious One. "He who overcomes, I will permit him to sit with me upon my throne; as I also have overcome and have sat with my Father on his throne" (Apoc. 3:21).

But another emphasis is equally important. If the relation of the Church to eternity is clear from the biblical tests, her responsibility to time and this world is hardly less insisted upon. Historically, the issue was clarified as early as the beginning of the gentile churches. Was the Church to experience temporal life and to be subject to the heavy pressures that history and events bring to bear upon mankind? The writings of the early communities reflect a consciousness both lucid and honest; the Church never conceived of herself as a sect of the illumined granted an exemption to stand outside the world of man. And the same question will always be relevant; it invades our present in a troubling way. Is not the Church responsible to man? And if she is, in what areas and to what degree? Or, to put the same question in another way, is the youthfulness of the Church to be understood as a transmigration of believers out of the actual world, an exemption from the human responsibility every man senses within himself? Is the gift of Christ a simple transcendence of the human condition? Is the youth of the Church no more than the untouchable youth of the pagan myths?

So long an experience in this world cannot but have supplied the Church with a clear answer to these questions. The evidence throughout history—the evidence of her teaching, of her work of mercy, of her intellectual presence, of her martyrs—is clear. She sees herself not as a youthful force standing at distance from mankind but as the juvenescence of mankind itself.

The grace of the Resurrection has enabled the Church to exercise a resurrecting power over all men. As the Body of the Lord, she was created a community sharing by faith in His victory. But her creation was no static or instantaneous event accomplished for the sake of twelve Jews, leaving mankind to go unchanged upon its dolorous way. Indeed, that former way, as Scripture makes clear, has passed away. "Behold, I make all things new" (Apoc. 21:5).

The early believers recognized in the Church a life continually given. Baptism and Eucharist are the sources of this life. The Lord's hand raised Christians from the despair and malice of unregenerate mankind, so that the Church herself has said to man with an absolute assurance, "Arise." This is her baptism, her first gift to mankind. And she brings the celebration of the death and victory of the Savior to her altars precisely because without food, man dies; he is subject to illness and death, his spirit is constantly threatened by the powers of evil. The sacraments of the Church in sum are the youthful vigor of Christ's divinity alive in her flesh and spirit, a vigor designed to heal, strengthen, restore, nourish, and unite. The sacraments are on behalf of man. This ancient principle is the key to the understanding of a Christian youthfulness that looks toward eternity and toward this world.

The sacramental life of a Christian, if we may come to a

formula, has as its purpose the creation of a Christian mind endowed with the world view of Christ Himself. The possession of this mind of Christ was, as St. Paul tells us, the early Christian boast—"we have the mind of Christ" (1 Cor. 2:16). And, again, he exhorts the gentile community, "Have this mind in you which was also in Christ Jesus" (Phil. 2:5). Paul speaks from the midst of the Church, equating the mind of the Church with the mind of Christ. Indeed, his thought indicates that the world view of Christ has passed over from Israel and the first communities into the Church of the nations.

We do well to pause over the reality of the "mind of Christ" that, in Paul's thought, has passed over into the mind of the Church. This sacred mind is, in fact, a very special insight with regard to the human community and the Father's will. The Father and mankind—these were the shaping forces that determined the vocation of the Word Incarnate. These two realities, the Father and mankind, indicated to Christ what Dostoevski has called simply the thing to be done! And the thing to be done, the experience to be undergone, was a death and a victory. In that passion and action, the mind of Christ took its final form. His world view, His special synthesis of all the elements of human existence—friendship, personal submission, the will to save, good and ill repute among men, the nobility and honor of being man—all these came to their great moment in His death and victory. Then the full experience of human life reached the Divine One with the force of a naked blow, both killing and resurrecting (Jn. 13:31).

But is one justified in concluding that this experience formed in Christ a mind that was restrictively religious? Is the Christ of eternal victory less human? The very opposite is true. Our faith assures us that the mind of the risen Christ is a passionate intuition, a profound insight into every element of man's struggle—a human life absorbed and elevated and given its final form. The Holy One assumed all in order to save all; now risen, He wears the marks of manhood that had been scored in his flesh as the price of love. And these same wounds mark Him as man forever.

"But we have the mind of Christ." In the Christian, the mind of Christ is a way of regarding the world, a way of being within mankind in the twentieth century. The Christic experience shapes a special world view; to be baptized is to undergo a radical transformation of the powers of one's mind. Through the sacrament, the Christian enters into man's corporate life in all its richness and hope and grandeur.

No one has ever called fidelity to the Christian experience an easy thing. Indeed, it has never before been so difficult to be a Christian, precisely because it has never before been so difficult to be human—to be aware of mankind, to stake one's life and energies on the future that is offered to all.

But the pain of human experience is undergone today not only by believers; it is not solely or even primarily the baptized who show themselves faithful to man's hope. In fact, one of the ironies of life today is that unbelievers are in many cases teaching new skills to Christian hands. Perhaps never before has there been a period when Christians have had so admirable a secular example. The fact is both heartening and discomforting. This is an age when unbelievers labor on behalf of mankind as though by a universal and mysterious social instinct. It is a time when national social programs have much in common with the teachings of papal encyclicals. It is a time when the law of the land is revised to meet the legitimate hopes of the

Negro, when that law, moreover, prods Catholics to speed up their own laggardly and unfinished business of integration in schools, parish churches, and hospitals.

Indeed, we are witnessing a strange rewriting of religious history, a phenomenon of little comfort to men who had thought of themselves as shapers of the world's conscience. The humiliating truth is clear: the life of the risen Christ is more pervasive and powerful than we had thought. In certain important aspects of life, in the formation of many attitudes that are deeply human, the youthfulness of Christ's mind has shown its presence not only in Catholic lives but also in many outside the visible Church. So we find Protestant communities who pray and work for Church unity, who take their stand in the front lines of the integration struggle, whose liturgical services are models of vitality and a sense of communion, whose missionary spirit runs strong and deep, who long and labor for the reign of Christ. A like sense of service and love is often verified in the Jewish community. And in devotion to the historic hopes of man and his social struggle, the secular humanists have outdistanced the Catholics in many areas, as we must admit.

We are being shown, in fact, that the youthfulness of the risen Christ is denied to the heartless, to the world-weary, to the coward, to the sacristy Catholic. This gift is denied all those who would make their own pride the determining measure of God's gift or who divorce the mind of Christ from the mind of mankind.

This youthfulness is marked, finally, by one great characteristic. Christian youthfulness is discernible by its breadth of mind. If man may be defined as the world grown conscious, the Christian mind is that world consciousness heightened. Indeed, men of real faith cannot conceive of themselves as existing out of this world, out of their own times, while still claiming to remain human or Christian. An invincible love of man is one of the deepest and most constant expressions of the Christian love of God. And the Christian sees this love of man as required of him by a simple and central truth.

His world, that is, is the gift-bearer of God. In sign and in reality, God has given himself through the things of the world, through its fires, guidance, horizon, and warmth, through its oils, healing, and strength. And this is not all. The gifts of this world are offered to men through human hands. The gift of material creation is thus an extension and symbol of the gift of the persons, of persons who welcome man, who feed and forgive him. Persons, finally, who by the central gift of all have led other men to one Person. And in one Man mankind finds both gift and giver, Father and Son and Holy Spirit.

The Providence of the Father in this world thus converges on Christ, for whom all things were made. Such a vision of life, at once organic and expansive, implies a large breadth of the Christian mind. Its sacred center is in Christ, in the sacraments, in the community of world, in the shape of life in all its unfinished innocence and mystery. All things, as the Christian mind realizes, are sacred; all reality, even its most hidden and unpromising elements, is a mysterious evidence of the Father's will made known in His Son, and throughout history it shapes a triumphant body of the Savior and the saved, of all men in one Man.

Thus Christian breadth of mind implies a passionate search for understanding. Man's glory is to search out the hidden meaning of events, with reverence not only for the mystery beyond but for the appearance at hand. The world, to this inward eye, leads from appearances into mystery. Both intuitive and synthetic, the Christian mind is the enemy of surface judgment and superficial opinion, enemy to the dissective process that destroys the living tissue of the Body of Christ by separating holiness from its human condition, history from divine intervention, social struggle from the Christian vocation.

But such a view of life exacts its cost. Many, even within the Church, prefer not to see. The battle against Christian insight is intensified in proportion as the things to be seen are unpleasant or unholy or unfamiliar. Beyond the ego, beyond affluence, beyond the secure and stable forms of life lies a world known only to those who wish to understand. It is a world of turmoil and crisis, of despair and injustice and grinding indigence. Christian insight knows it is there, but human selfishness has its own way of avoiding the issue. Somewhere between mind and hands, in the interval between judgment and action, men set up a delaying tactic.

In such a way, the fruit of wisdom is lost in double-talk, in prudential talk, or in untimely silence. And the moment passes that should have been the Church's moment. Its substance is seized upon by other hands and shaped to other uses; the moment is joined to a past and future that are deprived of Christian presence. By acts of refusal and cowardice, by the double-talk and delay of believers, time itself becomes consecrated to man without God; time becomes a secular phenomenon. Movements of history that were potentially sacred in their efforts toward the gospel ideal—their summons to justice and charity and human opportunity—such movements, meant in the plan of God to be Christian movements, have been gutted of their Christian spirit and rendered neutral, acrimonious, or anti-Christian. This has been true largely from the great revolutionary upheavals of the eighteenth century to the present world struggle of the emergent peoples.

With an almost inconceivable blindness, many Christians have served notice on the world that its struggles are its own affair; they are no affair of Christians as such. And the world by and large has acceded; it accepts that Christians prefer to live by another code than the Beatitudes. So the world has proceeded with its own temporal redemption.

When so massive and public a Christian failure occurs, two things immediately follow. In the first place, the movements of mankind in the direction of human solidarity, justice, and peace are diminished. They lose their best substance. It remains true that any movement on behalf of man, no matter what its nobility or greatness, can never be itself when it is consciously hostile to Christ or at distance from His spirit. And no Christian failure can invalidate this principle. At enmity with Christ, no human effort can call itself friend of man. No matter what it may accomplish in a human sphere, it cannot lead men to the transcendent freedom that Christ alone announces and confers. Deprived of His freedom, men still remain slaves, no matter what economic or political autonomy they may achieve. For the freedom of Christ is not in its substance the loosening of a specific human bondage at all; it is the release of man from the primordial slavery to sin and death, to the tyrannies of instinct and covetousness and lust. All human freedoms must, in fact, be the images, approaches, and preparations for this freedom that is God's gift. Apart from Christ, history shows that the loosening of human slaveries is inevitably marked by the ironic forging of new determinations—of the ego, of pride and hatred and envy. In such a way the liberators of men often become the masters of a new tyranny, and those who had begun to rejoice in their new freedom find themselves released only into a larger prison yard.

But when Catholics fail to serve the life of man, we must speak not merely of the loss to mankind that inevitably occurs. We must speak also of the loss to the Church. For it remains true that any loss of vitality and effortful love in the Church immediately affects those realities that are her human countenance and shape. She is the final form of humanity, so she must constantly give ear to the resonances of life, to man's hope as it takes shape from age to age; in the image of Christ, she must assume if she is to save. When the Church draws back or keeps at distance from movements of history, out of a questionable sense of the past or fear of change, she is, in fact, guilty of abstaining from mankind. Moreover, she is exacting of man what is morally beyond his forces. She is asking him to submit to her, without in any sense giving heed to him. She is suppressing or anathematizing human hopes, which are of such dignity that they often act as preambles of the faith itself. The preparation for the faith takes different forms at different times, as history shows; today, it often consists in a passionate love of justice and honor, in a rigorous consecration of man to the well-being of his fellow man. This is often the direct path by which modern men approach baptism. To turn man away from his aspirations in mankind or to ignore his struggles along that way is equivalent to undoing the preparation of God. It is to shunt man off in exasperation, in bitterness, or in despair—in search of a savior other than Christ.

To say that man must not be turned away is to insist once more that the Church is man's final hope—indeed, his only one. But in order that man may see the truth, in its simplicity and inner persuasive power, it must be made evident that the Christian faith does not make ghosts of living men. Unbelieving man seeks to know, in fact, whether the human drama, tragic, virile, and exigent, continues within Christian hearts. He will not easily resign being a protagonist in that drama; he has neither heart nor stomach for the role of the spectator, of the human neutral. He has no desire for a faith that anesthetizes conscience. He seeks, in fact, an adult community, a power of entering the real world ever more fully and deeply, in order to give the future of mankind a fuller and more noble form.

4. The Priesthood of the Laity

THE TRADITION OF the Church agrees that the nature of the priesthood, whether possessed by clerics or by the laity, is essentially social. One could mention many biblical sources here, among the most remarkable of which is surely the Letter to the Hebrews. The Letter speaks with a majestic sustained rhetoric of the priest Christ, a Being of divine power and of human compassion, doing the Father's work of reconciliation in the world. This Holy Priest is turned totally toward the Father and toward man; He is Son and Brother (Heb. 8:12). His acute sense of the Father's honor is verified on a human scene. He has taken the very shape of humanity to Himself and raised it to the dignity of priesthood in order to accomplish the work of restoration and peace in the human community (Heb. 5:14).

And the mystery of priesthood also has special emphasis in the writing of St. John. John formed his image of the Savior from the point of view of a Jewish liturgy that still awaited fulfillment. Humanity awaited its Priest. In Christ, men awaited their own destiny. Year upon year, century upon century, the long file of believing pilgrims made its way across history; the Exodus, the periods of prophets and kings extended the theme. Life was a religious venture, and sacrifice marked its great stages; sacrifices of burning and bloodletting formed a constant call upon the community to acknowledge its guilt and awaken its hope. In all these centuries, Jewish communities remained bitterly conscious of a double loss in mankind, a loss of sonship and of brotherhood.

These realities, sonship and brotherhood, were of the essence of man's life; they made man human. In the first days of existence, man had stood at that living intersection where he rejoiced in the dignity of being both son and brother—son to God, brother to his neighbor. This was the gift that God had offered man at the beginning of sacred history (Gen. 2).

But man had ruptured that bond. He had sinned and hidden away in the thicket; and when he was called, his answer already was redolent of arrogance, slavish fear, and double-dealing. "I was naked, and I hid myself" (Gen. 3:10). No longer son and brother, man had declared himself rebel and murderer.

The stain that infected man's dealing with God very shortly broke out into a universal human plague. The man who was rebel against God could not be friend to man. Rather, since he was God's enemy, his hatred of God corrupted the human community; it made of him the murderer of his brother. He committed a heinous crime against nature and against blood, effectively resigning his human love because he had already rejected his sonship in God. The murder of Abel was man's declaration of that war against man and God, the sin called original. "And the Lord said to Cain: Where is thy brother Abel? And he answered, I know not: am I my brother's keeper?" (Gen. 4:9).

The Savior would answer that question—and in blood. He had come to stand at the intersection of life, that place where man had struggled against God and murdered his brother. Christ had come to restore man at the crucial point of life where man had rebelled. He died and arose and left to mankind the effective commemoration of His love for them.

And in the Mass, God verifies once more the love which is older than man and which insists not only that man must love God but that without love of his brother, man is unworthy of the name human.

Human history reveals the truth again and again; the Mass dramatizes it in an entirely unique way. History insists on the unity of mankind, in its recurrent rhythms of anarchy and of harmony, of war and of peace. And it is to this history, to its tragic struggle and deferred hope, that the Mass summons believers. Through words and action, man is reminded constantly of the community task that awaits his hands and heart.

Men gain a true historic and human sense at the Eucharist. They are invited to contemplate a history that the Incarnation made sacred, once and for all. In His death and victory, the Son of God submitted to a process of life which man had profaned but which divine love had made sacred in the gift of Christ's life. The profane memory of mankind, stained with a history of revolt, has been cleansed by the action of Christ the Priest. "Having loved his own who were in the world, [Jesus] loved them to the end" (Jn. 13:1).

Men learn most vividly who Christ is by recalling what Christ has done. And they learn also in Christ's death and victory who they themselves are and to what they are called. So we recall, at the *memores* prayer immediately after the consecration, "the blessed passion of Christ our Lord, His resurrection from the dead, and His glorious ascension into heaven."

The prayer summons men to a new understanding of what has been brought to pass upon the altar. The death and the Resurrection of the Savior, made present under the banquet symbols, are dwelt upon in a sacred stillness, in gratitude and inner recollection. And the truth of this moment is not merely that our human memory is recalled to a past event, however noble and great. The Eucharist is not a mere memorial. Rather, by the power of God, our memories are immersed in a present happening—the celebration of Calvary and the Resurrection of Christ—at the sacrificial banquet. "We your servants and with us your holy people, recalling, making present your death and victory, do now offer you these holy gifts."

A view of life is opened before men here. It corresponds to history, to God's word, and to man's deepest instincts. Mankind is one in its members; mankind has fallen in one man, all have arisen in one Man, all go to God with one Man. So it is eminently true that to speak of the "social" character of the Mass is a pleonasm; it is like adding "social" to "Catholicism." It is as superfluous as adding "people" to "priesthood."

The priestly work of the people is in essence a work on behalf of a community. Christ had verified this. He was Son and Brother (Jn. 8:29). And His blood cried out to God more eloquently than the blood of Abel (Heb. 12:24). His blood was, in fact, creative of a race of sons and brothers. It bestowed a new reality on man; it gave man a new name in the Hebrew sense, in which a name strictly conforms to the reality and destiny of the person.

The new name of man would be adopted son of God. "Behold what manner of love the Father has bestowed upon us, that we should be called children of God" (1 Jn. 3:1). And the new name of man is also brother to man. "For this is the message that you have heard from the beginning, that we should love one another" (1 Jn. 3:11).

Now this work of reconciliation, the work of priesthood, is a work of God and a work of man. It is the very opposite of automatic or magical. It implies, rather, all the ironies and contrasts of a living historical process. Christ had finished the work, yet He had left it unfinished. He had assured its victory, yet He had placed it in the breach. Peace and unity are both accomplished in Him, yet they are left in continuing crisis. Reconciliation is possible, but for many it is not yet actual. The gift of God has been offered to man; it has not as yet been welcomed by all men (Heb. 2:11–17). The sorrows and difficulties that the Church is experiencing, and will always experience, in announcing the word of God to the nations bear witness to the essentially dynamic and temporal nature of salvation.

One must understand redemption as a continuing and unfinished work—as the work of the whole Christ. Certainly this was the understanding of St. Paul. Christians are mysteriously summoned by Christ to undertake a work that the divine plan for mankind has left unfinished. "What is lacking of the sufferings of Christ I fill up in my flesh" (Col. 1:24). And, again, "I bear the marks of the Lord Jesus in my body" (Gal. 6:17). The Savior has willed that the redemption of man be a vortex of a struggle that would mysteriously continue until the last day. In this way, the baptized are summoned, not to be static dispensers of formulas or the heralds of a victory that is finished with. To conceive of Christianity in such terms is to do injustice to its grandeur and challenge; it is to miss the human and historical substance of its work. It is to substitute a closed and magical system of salvation for an entirely open and unfinished history whose outcome still waits upon man's response to love as humanity struggles toward its fulfillment.

May we not say, then, that a biblical and eucharistic view of man implies all this—that the history of salvation is still open and that the Christian is still the shaper of man's history as Jesus was the shaper of history?

These are large words, and yet they express something extremely simple and lucid. We are suggesting that there is no substitute for the believer who is an unusual human being, permeated deeply with a sense of the life of man as man exists here and now. And this sense of sharing and shaping man's life comes to focus on the two great realities that are central to man's existence—sonship and brotherhood. Christianity is, in fact, the elevation and perfection of these crucial relationships of existence. The believer is by definition son of God and brother of man (Rom. 8:5).

This is the gift of God. What the Christian is empowered to announce and accomplish for others is already effectively conferred on the believer himself. As adulthood brings him new experiences, every human instinct assures him that he is son and brother of men, a relational being. Further, his baptism has intervened to bless and elevate these relationships, to make him son and brother in an entirely new way.

So through his human nature and through the gift of God, the Christian has entered into new relationships; his hope now is to introduce other men to the same realities. Man the rebel, the sinner, may look to the Christian and be healed, for the Christian is son of God. Man the solitary, the one who stands outside community for whatever reason, may look to the Christian in hope, for the Christian is lover of his brethren, brother to all, one who wears his humanity with a sense of power and weakness, of compassion and strength.

In their deepest hearts, do men seek anything else than a hope of healing and reconciliation? Let us suggest that the Christian is God's answer to the millennial search of man—a search for man and for God, a search that modern life has complicated and delayed to the point where men themselves can scarcely tell upon what road their feet lie.

An analysis of modern literature shows the breadth and purpose of this search. Man seeks his brother even in the denial of his brother. Graham Greene has probed the disease whose symptom is social refusal. One of his powerful and mordant short stories, "The Destructors," concerns a gang of London teenagers. Under the leadership of an architect's son, Trevor, they have decided on the destruction of a beautiful old house originally designed by Christopher Wren. The owner is absent; the destruction is in progress:

> "Come over here," Trevor said, "and look." Out of both pockets he drew bundles of bank notes. "Old Misery's savings."
>
> "What are you going to do? Share them?"
>
> "We aren't thieves," Trevor said. "Nobody's going to steal anything from this house. I kept these for you and me—a celebration. We'll burn them; one by one." And taking turns they held a note upwards and lit the top corner, so that the flame burned slowly toward their fingers. The gray ash floated above them and fell on their heads like age. "I'd like to see old Misery's face when we're through," Trevor said.
>
> "You hate him a lot?" Blackie said.
>
> "Of course I don't hate him," Trevor said. "There'd be no fun if I hated him." The last burning note illuminated his brooding face. "All this hate and love," he said, "it's soft, it's hooey. There's only things, Blackie," and he looked around the room crowded with the unfamiliar shadows of half things, broken things, former things. "I'll race you home, Blackie."

E. M. Forster and Aldous Huxley have seen the process of depersonalization as continuing at an accelerated rate, until man can no longer stomach man. In the world of the future the machine has won, and men and women are reduced to its image of impersonality and indifference. In Forster's short story "The Machine Stops," a woman is summoned to a television set to speak with her son in a far-distant country:

"Be quick, here I am in the dark wasting my time. . . ." ". . . Mother . . . I want you to come and see me. . . ." She watched his face in the blue plate. "But I can see you," she exclaimed. "What more do you want?" "I want to see you not through the machine," he said, "I want to speak to you not through the wearisome machine. . . . I see something like you in this plate, but I do not see you; I hear something like you through this telephone, but I do not hear you. That is why I want you to come. Pay me a visit, so that we can meet face to face, and talk about the hopes that are in my mind." She replied that she could scarcely spare the time for a visit. "The airship barely takes two days to fly between me and you." "I dislike air-ships." "Why?" "I dislike seeing the horrible brown earth, and the sea, and the stars when it is dark. I get no ideas in an air-ship!" "I do not get them anywhere else." "What kind of ideas can the air give you?" He paused for an instant. "Do you know four big stars that form an oblong, and three stars close together in the middle of the oblong, and hanging from these stars, three other stars?" "No, I do not, I dislike the stars. But did they give you an idea? How interesting. Tell me." "I had an idea they were like a man." "I do not understand." "The four big stars are the man's shoulders and his knees. The three stars in the middle are like the belts that men wore once, and the three stars hanging are like a sword. . . ." "It does not strike me as a very good idea, but it is certainly original."

But even in practical agnosticism, in desperate paganism, in the cult of pleasure and pride, there is a certain moral hope at work. It is the kind of recognition of illness that always wins mercy.

And let us not be overly pessimistic. The human situation is always saved by the few who retain conscience, hope, and a sense of man. It is of these Charles Williams speaks in *Descent Into Hell* (a poet, Stanhope, speaks to a troubled girl):

> "Haven't you heard it said that we ought to bear one another's burdens? . . . When . . . Christ said 'bear,' I think he meant . . . carrying a parcel instead of someone else. To bear a burden is to carry it instead of.
>
> ". . . If you insist on making a universe for yourself . . . if you want to disobey and refuse the laws that are common to us all, if you want to live in pride and division and anger, you can. But if you will be part of the rest of us, and live and laugh and be ashamed with us, then you must be content to be helped. You must give your burden up to someone else, and you must carry someone else's burden. I haven't made the universe and it isn't my fault; but I'm sure this is a law of the universe, and not to give up your parcel is as much to rebel as not to carry another's. . . . When you are alone, remember that I am afraid instead of you . . . and go on. Remember it is mine. . . ." Deliberately he opened himself to that fear. . . . The body of his flesh received her alien terror, his mind carried the burden of her world. The burden was inevitably lighter for him than for her, for the rage of a personal resentment was lacking; he endured her sensitiveness, but not her sin; the substitution there, if indeed there is a substitution, is hidden in the central mystery of Christendom.

Restoration is a work of both Christ and man. There is no exemption from the human burden, from the human glory, which is simply that one resolves to be open and vulnerable before life. In such a way, by an irony dear to the heart of God, the work of salvation is man's continuing task; it is not done with while time remains. And it continues in the power in which it began, in the shape which it first took—that is, in the priestly power of the baptized, in their sense of life, in their acute realization that to be a Christian is to assume the burden of being human. This sense of life, the sense of God and of man, would seem to be something more than a useful ascetical tool for the Christian. One would like to suggest that this double sense of existence, the sense of sonship in Christ and the sense of the human community, is simply the larger radiance of lay priesthood itself (1 Peter 2:9).

Every Christian senses this truth and rejoices in it. It is the heart of his effort, the source of his staying power and courage. He knows with Paul that he "can do all things in him who strengthens me" (Phil. 4:13). This grace makes him piercingly aware of standing at the heart of human life and of there carrying on the "admirable exchange," the commerce of God's mercy with man.

But if every Christian is son and brother, surely there are degrees of this grace and degrees of Christian response to it. Not every Christian, that is, is a great Christian. Some may be even minimal Christians, and many others only ordinary ones. And perhaps a hint of explanation of the modern Christian's failure to grasp and shape life may be found in the very reflections we are engaged in.

We might define a great or universal Christian as one who is endowed with three master attitudes or views of life. Such a believer is a man who longs for human unity, he is marked by a sense of his times, and he has a sense of the crucial nature of community action. Let us consider each of these in turn.

The merely good man's view of life is often untouched

by the longing that all men be one. The great Christian's view of life is unitive. The question here is, of course, one of degree. To grow too nice would be to destroy the whole value of the discussion, since there are almost infinite variations in temperament and views of Christian life. But one could say in general that the unusual Christian brings to bear on the realities of life a strongly unitive energy. To such a man, life is one, which is not to deny that it is complicated, perplexing, agonizing even. Still, such men as we speak of are able to sense the unity underlying Christian life, a unity of people and priest, of action and prayer, of secret decision and public work.

The spiritual life is a unity. The Christian stands firmly at the altar and in his world. He knows that the God of the altar is the God of the neighbor, that there are not several Christs in history, but one; and that this One wills to reveal and conceal Himself not only at the Mass but also in the mystery of man. (We recall that the word "communion" in its earliest use was a synonym for the body of the faithful.) And the Christian we speak of senses that the mysteries of altar and community must also be one in his heart. He refuses himself the luxury of a restrictive sense of Christ. If he is fervent and exact and serious at the altar, he is fervent and exact and serious among men. In both cases, a mystery has engaged his sense of reality. He comes to know that the eucharistic sacrifice accomplished at the altar is not finished when the missal is closed. The Eucharist, in fact, prolongs itself in the neighbor. A eucharistic work is continued by Christians in man's flesh and mind. The nourishment of the bread and the word continues in corporal works, in counseling and forgiving, in the effort to purify and elevate human existence at every point.

In such a way, by the will to unity and by work on its

behalf, all the elements of Christian life enrich one another. Through the apostolate, a believer's sense of God is deepened. The works of mercy save the man who performs them; they save his human sense from becoming vaporized or abstracted out of this world. They give character and concreteness to his love. Through Christian service, man shares that sense of human life that one notes in the heart of Christ. And when such a Christian comes to the altar, he does so with the needs of men impinging on his heart. All men stand with him there. He pleads for them—not for an abstract flock or a remote people of history, an ideal people, a sinless people, but for the actual people of God, the ignorant and unconvinced and desperate and unhappy ones, those whose faith is a lifelong struggle, whose Christianity has little of triumph or the spectacular about it. The widest possible sense of human life makes of the life of worship a redemptive and priestly and human experience.

In this way Christian worship tends to merge with a Christian sense of man. One ventures to say that the Christian comes to know his community most truly at the altar; there he learns man's true condition in a way he can learn it nowhere else. And the knowledge is simply this. The work of priesthood is, in its vastly greater part, a mystery, and it shares in the darkness and unknowability of the cross (1 Cor. 1:21). Man's victory is in hope; and his hope, in order to vindicate itself from the stain of earthly hope, has sometimes to be pushed to the point of absurdity. The Christian must hope on like Abraham, "hoping against hope" (Rom. 4:18). And he can come to some understanding of this only at the altar, where the priesthood of Christ acts in his own action, where Christ offers in his offering, where Christ's victory blesses his struggle.

At the altar, the Christian comes to know that Christ

saved when Christ was powerless. At an hour when earthly hopes were extinguished and man had come to know the depths of his impotence, at such an hour, God chose to save. And the divine healing still awaits the acknowledged helplessness of man; in order to be cured, our sickness must grow worse.

And when we come to consider Christian virtue, we find in great Christians a like search for unity and integration. There are in the true Christian no extremes or distraction or inner violence but, rather, a quiet intensity and balance. Such a man does not fear to expose his heart to the scrutiny of man and to the scrutiny of Christ. He knows beyond doubt that a life of prayer, of poverty of spirit, and of charity is a requirement of the Christian life, and he goes forward in this way. He has a strong conviction that he cannot be one man in secret and another in public and still be man of Christ. He knows, indeed, that personal decisions have a way of rewarding or exacting revenge on man and that the Christian who is secretly resolved on mediocrity, personal comfort, ambition, or the cult of the ego will blunt or even amputate his contribution to the public life of man. The mediocre Christian will inevitably use his powers with clumsiness or cowardice; his language will be fumbling; he will even give up presenting a high ideal before others; he will be unable to offer that silent and unremitting example to the lives of Catholics that can induce Christian and human adulthood in them.

We spoke of the Christian as marked by a strong sense of the present and of his world. We must make our terms quite clear. There is no question here of the man whose sense of the present is a rather crude involvement in the affluent life and its gadgets and games or in intellectual childishness. A Christian's sense of the times is nothing so flimsy or artificial as this. We are thinking, rather, of a sense of this world that is like Paul's. Such a sense of the times takes its lead from the Incarnation of the Son of God. It may be called an affective and intellectual friendship with man's world. This sense of reality is a conviction that the divine is friend to man, that grace is the immersion of human life in the life of God.

In speaking this way, one must be conscious of a full sympathy for differing temperaments and views of life. The heart and mind of the Church are as ample and generous as the heart of Christ; she accepts all men, as He did. And it is true that conservatism is fostered by many elements of modern life. Many Christians, materially fortunate, live and die with the implicit belief that the life they have known is the common lot of mankind. No least suspicion is aroused in them that their lives have been highly special in a material sense, that they have been favored in ways that most men never experience.

It is not to be thought wonderful that such people will also have a restricted experience of the faith and will tend to conclude that their experience of the Church coincides rather exactly with reality. Their lives, so safe and protected, encourage them to think that the faith is finished, academic, a matter of formulas and of legal observance. Such men will consider themselves as certainly obligated to God and only possibly obligated to mankind. And they will think of faith and the human order as necessarily separate realities.

We note in many Christians, as a result of such influences, a certain remoteness from life, a tendency toward indecision, a distrust of individual opinion except if it is official opinion, a strong bias toward the prudential, a quick skill at detecting the vagaries of modern life and a corresponding blindness in regard to its values, a strong sense of the dogmatic and a correspondingly weak sense of the pragmatic, a tendency to enlarge the areas of clerical competence and to restrict areas of lay competence.

Let us reflect on this remoteness from life, especially one aspect of it that seems particularly regrettable today— the lack of sympathy in the minds of priests for a truly adult social apostolate. It is an indifference to life's forms perhaps related to the conviction that the sacred must be kept immune from the issues of this world. So most sermons preached in the modern Church stress the dogmatic or moral or personal formation of layman but leave them with hardly any cause to reflect on public life and Christian involvement.

There is something more here, one would think, than an unrealistic view of the layman's powers of thought. It is not simply a question of priests' remaining silent on public moral issues because they think the layman ought to draw his own conclusion within his own life. To speak bluntly, the social order is sometimes neglected in the public speech of the Church because to draw social conclusions from Catholic moral teaching would be uncomfortable and disturbing and because in the minds of many priests, prudential judgments rule almost any given circumstance. It is thought somehow unworthy of holy Church that she should mix in conflict; it disturbs good order, disturbs good men, and awakens ugly local feeling and controversy. It puts the Church in the breach; it makes her, the mother of peace, a source of friction and hatreds. For all these reasons, in many dioceses of the South, for example, the patent conclusions of the doctrine of the Mystical Body are ignored. Priests walk a gingerly path around local and obvious facts. Prudence wins out. It wins out not only against unwise zeal and extremism but also against charity, against public scandals, against the feelings and consciences of Negro Catholics, who are in many cases left to fend for themselves when faced with a conspiracy of silence or procrastination. In such a way, public and personal wrongs perpetuate themselves within the Church.

And to speak of the North, the situation is not startlingly different. From the silence which up to recent times has veiled many pulpits in regard to social questions, Northern Catholics are free to draw many conclusions. One of them would say, "We of the North have no Negro problem; if we did, the priests would speak of it." Giving the lie to this are northern Negro slums and Catholic real-estate owners and employers who draw as hard and fast a line across the Negro path as was ever drawn in the Deep South, forbidding them areas of housing and work.

This failure of courage in facing one's own times, this lack of a full-blooded sense of history, inevitably harms the Church's efforts in many ways. Let us speak of two forms of that harm. First, from the point of view of conversions, the clear apologetic always evident in a body of vigorous, honest men is blurred into an ambiguous picture of Catholic safeness, of false peace, and of jargon. And men today are unerringly aware of this; especially aware are the men who would make the best Catholics. They are simply not drawn to a Church that seems to dwell with unfeeling detachment in the midst of turbulence and injustice, a Church that assures herself and her believers, by implication or silence, that all will be right if we keep our heads and stay clear of messy conflict. Such thinking, or such a presentation of what the Church is, stands as far from the gospel as it does from the thought of men like Leo XIII and Pius XII and John XXIII. Such cowardice is, in effect, a bargaining for a false peace that has no place in the war for man's soul.

And in consequence of our failure to be true to the peace of Christ and to bear with Him the cross of public, courageous action, it often happens that valuable men remain outside the Church. Such men and women do not see in Catholics that fire which the Savior came to light upon the earth. Rather, they find in us a stereotype of some of the least valuable qualities of those who claim no faith at all; we are, they say, safe and institutionalized and predictable.

And failure of social action in the Church performs still another disservice to her. It is a commonplace to hear priests mourning that Catholics are apathetic in regard to the whole Christian pattern of life. Our parishioners can hardly be persuaded to reflect, to pray, to read, to converse with any degree of seriousness. The sensory life of the world seems to swallow them whole. They largely pursue the same values as others, they love and hate with the loves and hates of this world. And even when they are persuaded into some form of Catholic Action, it is often in a childish or protesting or moralistic way.

Now, this situation of the Church will be part of the lifelong struggle of the good Christian. His Church will never be free from the lax, the indifferent, even the scandalous. But let us add that when one has agreed to a truth, he is still far from the whole truth. The whole truth about the sterility and neutralism of much of modern Catholic lay life must include the priest in its picture. And the priest's part in all this brings us back to our reflections on a truly Catholic sense of life, a sense of vitality, an understanding of men today, a passion to reach and affect other lives. It remains true, for good or for ill, that laymen take their lead from their priests, that they are men of wisdom or men of blindness in general accord with the vision of life held out to them by their priests.

One reason, surely, why laymen are somewhat childish in understanding the faith is that many priests are dogmatists. The faith is often preached as though the congregation were made up either of theologians or of children. So laymen fail to sense the meaning of Catholic life or to understand their part in its processes. And this remains sadly true because the form in which they receive the faith is sometimes neither adult nor human. It is rather consistently abstract, moralistic, and apart from man's life.

But man, as St. Thomas says, in both *mens et manus*—he has intelligence and hands. If we give his hands nothing to do, his mind falls to sleep or grows bored or is reassured in its worst assumptions—that the Christian has no task, no responsibility to grow or to love, that the mind can be Christian and the hands remain idle.

We are forced by the nature of things to conclude that priestly courage is the father of lay courage, that a sense of life in the pulpit engenders a layman's sense of life in public. Further, it is clear that when man's thinking does not engage man's hands, two things tend to happen—his hands soften and lose their skills, and so does his thought.

And this brings us to our final reflection on modern lay life as it relates to the life of the priest. The fact is that many priests continue to remain at a distance from adult lay life and its growing capabilities for serious Christian action. There are many signs that this is true, and one can do little more than point to them and leave conclusions to those who seek a change. One thing that strikes many observers is the rather constant rate at which the apostolic ambitions of college graduates tend to level off five or ten years after graduation from college. Active, zealous men and women, highly trained and presumably ready for parish leadership and community work, are simply never heard from during their adult productive years. It is being said by many adult Catholics with increasing bluntness that parish organizations are lifeless, that they offer no intellectual or spiritual formation, that the tasks they undertake are merely appendages of the clerical will.

Another straw in the wind is the undeniable truth that some twenty-five years after the lay apostolic movements began in this country, they are still waging an uphill battle for clerical approval and help. This is true of the Catholic Family Movement, the Young Christian Workers and Students, the Legion of Mary, the revitalized sodalities. And the fault cannot be imputed altogether, or even primarily, to the laymen; it lies in largest measure with priests who have shown small understanding and will to work with the adult energies of the baptized.

As a result of these conditions, a twenty- or thirty-year gap has opened in the ecclesiastical life-span of the average layman. He is strongly supported by his Church throughout childhood and adolescence. He is schooled, given the sacraments, counseled, shriven, and confirmed in his faith. But from the ages of twenty to fifty, years that from both the human and the Christian points of view must be considered as man's most productive period, the layman is usually adrift as far as his Church is concerned. He is not heard or welcomed or put to serious work; he goes about his own business. Finally, he reappears again, usually domesticated and set in his views, to join a parish organization geared to the onset of old age. But his best and most creative years, what of them? They are, by and large, a story of loss, of leakage, and of compromises. They are also years that from the point of view of man's life in God have been lived at subsistence level, without serious help or challenge or direction from priests.

And this situation continues in spite of the great varieties of lay apostolates today. Given the better education and human opportunities of Catholics, our laymen are prepared to take on great burdens and handle them with dispatch and professional skill. These burdens would include the social needs of mankind both at home and abroad, the great political challenge of the emerging nations, the needs of the poor, the educational needs of Africa and Latin America and the East.

In the face of these evident worldwide needs, priests continue to act and think as though parish life, continued in a deadly traditional way, could awaken the intelligence and competence of Catholics. Such thinking can only engender bitterness and disillusionment in the Body of Christ.

The solution would seem to lie in the general admission that no parish today can be itself without going beyond itself. The parish produces greatness in its own people by enlarging their horizons to the point where they embrace the world in its truth, complexity, need, and hope. In the process, the parishes of the developed nations contribute human greatness to the Church at large, to the lay missions, to the intellectual world, to the many forms of the extraparochial apostolate.

Another interesting aspect of our present situation is the fact of the layman's status symbols. One notes how priests and laymen alike have created and maintained them; views of lay prestige, subtly reflected in the attitudes of priests, help or hinder laymen to understand themselves and to be themselves. By and large, as contemporary life shows, clerical response to lay status coincides nicely with the attitudes of our culture. Priests respect those professions that are rewarded and respected by Americans today. And this is not necessarily a bad thing; doctors, lawyers, Catholic professional men have done admirable work for their communities. One can admit this and still insist that to defer to professional men—as always and everywhere the first to be heard, to be worked with, or to be given responsibility in the Church—is at best a restrictive view. One is allowed to doubt whether such an attitude corresponds to the needs of the Church here and now. Laymen who are heard from and whose attitudes prevail in the Church should not primarily or automatically be those who have "arrived" in a restricted material or professional area of life. Otherwise, the Church risks nothing and attains no breadth; she reflects only the social attitudes and methods of men who tend to be self-protective, ruggedly individualistic, and resentful of change.

It is becoming more and more evident that the layman's development simply will not occur without the priest's help. If such development does occur on its own, by main force of lay conviction, it does so at the price of balance. Isolated lay life is marked by defensiveness; it loses the sense of peace, acceptance, and achievement that is its right. And if we have cause to mourn the fact that some lay movements are not as Catholic as they might be, that laymen are more critical than helpful, that they see only fault and defect in the Church, our own criticism stick in our throats. The question is, rather, why was priestly influence lacking at the beginning and all along the course of lay development?

One could pass many instructive hours considering papal documents in this regard. They invariably converge on a rather revolutionary but very old and deeply Christian idea. Over the past four hundred years, an untapped reservoir of intelligence, courage, enterprise, and action has been allowed to rise, slowly and mightily. This reservoir is the energy of millions of baptized men and women. No one, or almost no one, thought to tap it, to canalize it, to channel it to its mighty potential. One is tempted to ask, considering the centuries of Christian loss and conflict from the Reformation to the First World War, why these laymen's energies were not put to use. Why were no laymen on the foreign missions? Why were laymen not conducting universities and schools? Why were they not writing theology and philosophy and apologetics? Why were they not instructing the ignorant? Why were they not articulate in public life, in politics, in writing, in the social and political upheavals that have shaped mankind?

And the answer would be, possibly and clumsily, that history was not ready for them. The Church was not ready. Perhaps even the laymen himself was not ready. And the answer would stand as long as the question was cast merely in historical terms and left at that.

But alter the question and the answer is valueless. Put in present terms, the question "Why is the layman not taking his adult, responsible place on the Church's team today?" cannot be simply put off with "Because the Church is not ready" or "Because the times are not ripe."

The times are ripe to the point of falling to the one who will reach and pluck them. And the times have for their spokesman all our recent Popes. According to them and according to the ground swell which is rising daily and yearly in the Church and which anyone gifted with sight can see, the layman is ready. He is ready in impressively large numbers and with even more impressive capability and zeal. It is no longer a matter of the pioneering effort of a few, of this or that voice in the wilderness. History has reached flood tide. The opportunity is at hand today for both priest and layman to ride and harness the crest.

Priests today who have a sense of the Church know that the Church is fully herself only when the layman's adult voice is heard. Such priests will labor to bring the layman to adulthood, will encourage him to speak, will bear with his fits and starts, his clumsiness, the mistakes that always accompany awakenings. The enterprise we speak of is surely one for men of unusual love and of unusual capacity for courage and suffering. Such men, priests and laymen both, "will be forgiven their mistakes," Cardinal Suhard assures us. They will be forgiven because all their mistakes, reckoned over a lifetime at compound interest by their harshest critics, still will not equal the one error that alone is mortal and final—the error of inaction, somnolence, and false peace.

Those who resist change in the Church become the enemy of the Church they serve. We may be willing to pay any price to prevent mistakes in the Church, but the price we pay for peace may be the costliest mistake of all. The peace we cherish may be a false peace; if it is, its outward signs will be sterility and stagnation. To cherish this false peace is to violate both nature and grace. A law common to both realities decrees that to neglect the development of life energies or to forbid their development to others is to court personal and social ruin. And to refuse the Church the best energies of her own members, out of a false sense of proprietorship or clerical egoism, is to wound the Church at her very heart.

5. Sacred Art and the Life of Man

RECENTLY, MANY GOOD minds have been calling attention to tendencies in modern life that distract men from the realities of life itself. We are warned by analysts of our culture that the visual media are acting like giant dream machines, churning out an unlimited stream of fallacy, unreality, and soporifics. The dangers inherent in the creation of this limitless dreamworld are ominous enough. But perhaps only another Orwell could picture their horrific triumph—the day when the dream had won out in a world inhabited by the fastidious, the fearful, and the sterile.

I should like to suggest that the Catholic universe also has its subworld of the dream, that the symptoms and stimulants of this dream are largely at hand, and that a crucial Catholic postulate is being variously endangered and weakened by the onset of the dream. I refer to the Catholic postulate that underpins our worship, our moral code, our hardy sense of time and eternity—I would call it simply the summons bidding the Catholic to search out and assimilate reality, to have a kind of passion to be vitally present to things as they are.

The world of religious art would seem to offer a good point of departure for a discussion of the Catholic dreamworld. The advantages of even a brief examination of Christian art history in this regard are apparent. Historically, the art of the Church was for extended periods of time a prime shaper of the Catholic sense of reality. Christian art at its best invited believing men into a deepened sense of existence; it made use of certain noble, easily recognized figures to remind believers that the faith was a virile, exigent summons into reality.

By way of beginning, one notes that the mysteries that this art dealt with were the very opposite of a surrogate for reality. They were, in fact, reality in depth. Inviting man to contemplate certain pivotal events of his sacred history, they also invited him to continue those events in his own life. The mysteries were to become the very form of man's soul; he was, in the strictest sense, to become what he contemplated—mind and heart and imagination were to bring about the assimilation of the icon in human life. Then, it was understood, this process of visual integration would have its logical flowering. The Christian would radiate in his world the holy energies that lay powerfully within the Christian mysteries and their expression—energies that awaited release through faith, worship, and sacrificial love.

This summons to man had its negative side too. Sacred art forbade to believers the detours, the ambiguities, and the profane games of the pagans. It forbade men to veer off into the empyrean or the daydream. It set before them, rather, a vision of life which God had joined and which man was forbidden to cut asunder; it commanded that this vision become man's vision—a union of action and contemplation, of time and eternity, of flesh and spirit, of God and man.

This view of life, dramatized in Church art, came to its focus in the art of the basilica apse. Apsidal art, summing up as it did the Church's view of existence, stands at the heart of the present discussion. For it was here, in her sanctuary images, that the Church spoke most eloquently of her name, her task, and her Lord.

In general, a rather large concave space of wall rose behind and above the altar and terminated in a great round arch. The idea that determined the handling of this space was the eucharistic mystery. The artist was to visualize one or another aspect of the sacred banquet of the Lord—the upper room, the Resurrection, Pentecost and its Apostles, the victorious Lord. But this was not all; dramatizing the Mass in art almost invariably meant that the sacrificing community was itself portrayed. So in this apse area, powerful mosaics and frescoes came into being, picturing the Church in triumph and the Church on earth. These images were conceived, in fact, as interpretations of the Mass action; they showed forth two stages of the Church—the community of holiness that the Eucharist was in process of forming and the celestial community of the last day.

In the lower horizontal space, the Church militant was a frequent theme. Sometimes the Twelve Apostles were pictured, sometimes the saints of a local liturgy. But no matter what personages were chosen, the artist made it clear that these ideal types were men and women of time. Their feet were planted on earth. They bore the tools of responsibility and service—keys of office, books, the vestments of priesthood, instruments of martyrdom. The implication was clear. Christian life in this world honored human realities; indeed, it was built up of them. The bodies of men, their human vocations, the life of the mind, creative instincts that expressed themselves in literary and scientific work—all these moved upward from this world in rhythms strongly expressive of the Church's approval of life.

And this was no otherworldly statement, to be put away in theological treatises. The Christian attitude toward time and human life was courageously stated in sacred

art by men who had sensed these things powerfully and
sensuously and whose intuitions the Church guarded as
the apple of her eye—the eye that has in it neither
mote nor beam. By placing the images of great men in her
sanctuary, the Church was warning believers against the
threat of the Gnostic dream.

In its simplest terms, this dream might be called a
separatist sense of eternity. The dream tempts believers to
pass through this world with sterile hands and minds. Such
a vision of things is bound to be the enemy of the art we
speak of; its illusions cannot bear with the Church's large
and pervasive sense of continuity, a sense that holiness
proves itself under pressure, a sense whose art places
celestial men and women in an earthly setting and bids
the faithful approach and learn from them the meaning
of life. Understanding that time and eternity were firmly
distinct realities, the Church would not allow their realities to be separated to the point where Gnosticism could
effect a divorce between them. God had joined time and
eternity. The two were one, and the name of their holy
juncture was Christ. In His image, His great icon, Christians would explore the profound connaturality that joined
the Church militant to the saints.

When reality has been courageously presented, there is
no end to the resonances that it starts in the heart of man.
This early Church art, supremely realistic and firmly
based in human life, had within itself the power of forming in believers a master idea toward time and this world.
By way of contrast with the dreamworld, we might call
this attitude a sense of the essential unity that underlies
human life.

The early Church, drawing upon the rather recent presence of Christ among men, had sensed strongly the unitive achievement He had brought to pass. In Him, the

Divine had blessed all stages and processes and forms of
man's life. The Lord had come not only to heal the rupture
of sin but to enter and bless those areas of life that even
redeemed man is slow to call holy. The blessing of
Christ's presence lay on work and recreation and marriage,
on the thought and love of man, on man's body and senses
and passions. The blessing was both cosmic and personal;
it reached deep into man's existence to declare the meaning of man.

And it was this Figure of triumphant benediction that
crowned the great social scene of the early apse. Christ
had brought the Church into being and had taken His seat
at the right hand of the Father. He is Christ of the theology of St. Paul and of St. John, the Kyrios, the Lord of
history. His countenance is suffused with a powerful
majesty, a consciousness that spans the universe of time
and human decision and awaits tranquilly the hour when
He will return to claim the universe He had won with His
blood.

But the Lord does not merely sit apart from men, from
life, from the decisions that are shaping time. Even in
eternity, He is mindful of man; He bears man's wounds
in hands and feet and side. Although He has ascended,
He is still with us. He is the great Priest of the heavenly
liturgy; with a moving pride and joy, He bears the marks
of His belonging to man. Alpha and Omega, the beginning
and the end, Victor over sin and death—He is all this. But
also, as the whole form and rhythm of the icon and its texts
make clear, He remains immanent in human life. The
words that surround the early frescoes and mosaics speak
of His presence with a sober courage and joy. They remind man, on the one hand, of the absolute triumph already won. But they are also a reminder that the fullness
of the Lord's victory awaits the achievement of men—their

acceptance of Christ, their acceptance of the brethren and of the shape of life itself. The good news of Christ is of a victory—but the victory cannot emerge in its full splendor in a regressive, adolescent world. It awaits the adult response of man.

The qualities of this early image of Christ make it supremely serviceable in the formation of the community. The qualities have already been mentioned; the Christ of the primitive Christian imagination was adult, and He was victorious.

Long before the icon had reached the grandeur of the seventh century, the Church had pondered the evidence of St. Paul telling who this Christ was. Mysteriously, Paul had linked an "age" of Christ to an "age" of Christians. He has spoken of the "mature measure" of the adulthood of Christ (Eph. 4:13) and had gone on simply to identify this Christic adulthood with the maturity of the believing Church.

As the form of the icon developed, it remained profoundly true to this intuition. It pictured a community assembled around Christ, a community that was coming to maturity in time. And this maturity was a matter of achievement that men everywhere could recognize. It had been won by intellectual distinction (the Fathers of the Church) or by a decision that arose from a profound resonance with the heart of the Church—a decision that had, in fact, cost men their lives (the martyrs). And the crown of this human adulthood was Christ.

At one stroke, His death and victory had brought the race of men from its millennial childhood into the mature world. His manhood and its gift were a summons to manhood. But it was more than that. He was Himself the Icon, the exact and luminous Image, of what it means to be man. He was Truth and Love—and here was man's clue.

But He was more, even, than this. His gift to man had been more than an exemplarity, however noble. It was a mysterious and sacred energy, the substance of Pentecost. "You shall receive power" (Acts. 1:8). The life of the risen Christ, vitalizing the community, had stirred minds and hearts to the point where adulthood had been actualized in all men; they could now know the truth and abide in love. Man was adult for the first time in his tortured history. He was himself, through the grace of Christ.

We are justified in saying that adulthood has been reached in human life when the person is in viable touch with reality, when the values, truth, and beauty of existence have been acceded to. In the psychological and religious worlds, the adult moves spontaneously toward things as they are. And being in touch with reality, he finds sufficient reason to choose. He knows, indeed, that reality commands him to choose, that without choice his grasp on reality petrifies. So he comes to choices that are true, in the deepest sense, to man and to God; they are true to that shape which Providence gives to the life of man in a given period and which decrees that man will live not in ideal or perfect times but in his own times. Adult man can face this shape of things with the countenance of adulthood, with love, concern for others, intellectual aliveness, an edge of good humor.

The early art of the Church indicates strongly that from the beginning, the religious sense of the community had had this sense of time, community, altruism. The choices of believers must favor God and the neighbor. And these choices had their master image—the choice of Christ. In His death, He restored the broken order of the moral universe, by an act of loving obedience offered to the Father. And this act had had incalculable effects on the human community. Because it was made by a Man, in favor of all men, this act of love created a universe in which the love of God and the love of one's fellow men became a principle of life.

This image of the adult Christ and its impact on the sensibility of the early Church raise questions that are central to man's life today. Religious psychology indicates that men never enter easily into adulthood. They resist the deepening of consciousness, the loneliness, the sense of crisis implied in growth. They tend, even in religious matters, to cling to "the things of a child" (1 Cor. 13:11). Along their religious journey, they are tempted time and again to regress to childhood and its comforts and peace. And if they are believers, they tend to seek approval for these regressive urges in the religious images they surround themselves with.

Many such images strike one as a massive form of resistance against the threat and demands of maturity. They stress the childish, the comforting, the soft. Their lines and colors have little to do with austerity, decision, growth. Rather, they bless man's childish quest for a religious ideal that is strictly out of this world. Such images invite him to no real Christ, to no real neighbor, to no real sense of time or of this world. They allow no suspicion to reach man that Christianity is a matter of deeds, even of one's blood. They are powerless to remind man that until adult energies stand "in service," offered to Christ under a mysterious Providence of time and the human community, a man may well be pious or upright, but he is not yet Christian.

Implicitly such religious images deny that Christianity is a religion of process, meant to bring man through stages of life to a matured sense of responsibility, to a sense of his times and his communities. In one or another way, they canonize childhood. They lay heavy hands on a life that is, in the nature of things, temporary and preparatory, and they hypostatize this state, projecting it into a Christian "ideal." And around the childish image, like withered flowers in dry vases, lie the tired virtues of childhood, once fresh and vigorous. Obedience has withered into passivity and inertia of will. Confidence in others, spontaneity, a sense of the newness of life have grown old and fallen away. They could not outlast childhood in the form in which they had graced the child; they were meant to issue into the rooted, hardy realities of self-confidence, balanced judgment, the willingness to bear the burdens of other men. And when they could not grow, they died.

The images we speak of are powerless to lead the Christian into his adulthood. They lead him, rather, into a life that never was, on land or sea. And their childishness and the childishness they induce contrast sharply and ironically with the world in formation around the Christian. It is the real world, the only world man has. It is a world that calls out to the Christian and invites him; its voice is an adult one, a voice of pain and sorrow and sin. It is a world of crisis—in personal decision, in marriage, in neighborhoods, in its cultural and political ferment. And in such a whirlwind, the regressive can never be a source of decision or of trust. He can be only a victim, a tourist, or a misfit.

A second great characteristic of the early icons of Christ marked Him invariably as Victor. This emphasis meant that the symbol of the cross, when it appeared at all, was absorbed in His triumph. So from the third to the seventh centuries, we find the cross introduced only to emphasize in its gold and jewels the radiance of Christ's achievement. All the literalness of the images we are familiar with, their stress on the anatomical and the agonizing, is wholly absent.

But to speak only of the figure of the Savior, His image undergoes an interesting artistic development during these early centuries. In the most primitive images, He appears in a youthful, rather characterless guise borrowed from the Roman country myths. But the Christian imagination found its own ground rather quickly. By the seventh century, the image had matured, aided no doubt by the encounter between the victory data of Scripture and the favorable course of history. So the Christ of Ravenna and the Pantocrator of Sicily and Byzantium came into being. In every case, He was the Victorious One, whose victory shed its holy radiance on the Church.

There is much more to this development than an interesting Christian footnote. Rather, everything native to the Christian sense, beginning with the witness of the Apostles themselves, insists that this art is deeply right, that the victory of Christ is central to Christianity. Convinced of this, believing men and women from the first ages of the faith offered their energies to a cause that they were certain would emerge out of pain and travail and death into the light. Their lives expressed the most sublime conviction that their efforts were joined to the victory of the Lord and, through Him, assured the eventual victory of all men.

And the Savior had shown how deeply rooted is this human longing for triumph. His gaze was never long arrested by death. His final word was one of triumph—"It is consummated" (Jn. 19:30). And so, in undismayed knowledge of the Father's Providence, He died. And the height and breadth of His victory are understandable only from the vantage point of the depths of His defeat. Ideal Man of history, He endured the malice of man to its bitterest depths. No declivity of suffering could remain unexplored by Him. He must bring to human life and to its outcome the fullness of human and divine gifts, and allow them to be tested in that darkness. For unless death and sin poured their malice upon Him, His victory would lack the riches and substance that man's hope leads him toward—the awareness man seeks, even in his God, of what it is to be man.

The art of the early centuries implies an understanding of all this. It dramatizes the great victory hymn of the early Church, quoted by Paul in his Letter to the Christians at Philippi. Both poetry and art opened before men the divine logic, the eternal "therefore" that joined the death of Christ to His victory and to the victory of all men:

> He humbled himself,
> becoming obedient to death,
> even to death on a cross.
>
> Therefore God also has exalted him
> and has bestowed upon him the name
> that is above every name,
>
> so that at the name of Jesus
> every knee should bend of those in heaven,
> on earth and under the earth,
>
> and every tongue should confess
> that the Lord Jesus Christ is
> in the glory of God the Father. (Phil. 2:8–11)

These data of Scripture and their portrayal in early art strike one as forming the center of early Christian consciousness. And one cannot but question whether the sense of victory we speak of—a sense of Christ's triumph and of man's irreplaceable part in its fullness—is not quite generally lacking to men today. We believe much more readily in defeat than in triumph. So our acceptance of per-

sonal and social mediocrity as a state of Christian nor-
malcy is matter of course and quite generally unexamined.
We take failure as part of the Christian scheme of things,
when in fact it often proceeds from simple cowardice and
lack of effort. We do not expect Christians to succeed in
important human enterprises; we have little idea of a
Church that, as a matter of course, encourages and stimu-
lates human greatness. We are content to leave achievement to others and to justify our poor showing in the name
of theology or asceticism; we are too busied, we imply
airily, about the one expedient thing. And when a Catholic
does come to eminence in some area of life, we are sur-
prised and even irritated. We sometimes speak as though
he must have won his prize at the price of "pure" Christianity, by a compromise of the gospel.

And our favorite modern image of Christ, the mass-
produced crucifix, can even be "used" to bless the view of
life we speak of. The image itself is often garish, overly
humanized, and artistically worthless. The Savior it por-
trays is undergoing an agonizing death or is already dead.
The body is anatomically rendered, often with a tendency
toward the feminine in color and line. It is an image of
the death of a good man—and of nothing more; as such,
one is justified in naming it a visual heresy.

The devotional art of the Stations of the Cross, when
these images of the suffering Savior are weak and sentimental, tend to extend and codify the death image
throughout a Passion sequence. In it, the death of the
Savior is brought, step by step, to its logical conclusion—
the believer is left with a buried Christ, entombed and
defeated. Such images generally allow no hint to come
through of the Divine Hero who arose and ascended to
the Father and whose luminous body is the master image
of our own victory.

The fact that the image of the Crucified is universally cherished by Christians is certainly not a point of discussion here. Throughout history, great saints and lowly hidden Christians have found in the sufferings of Christ their source of courage as they took up the burdens life imposed on them. A Christian consciousness, admirably balanced and constant, has in this way shed a measure of light on the way all men must go, on the realities every man must face; and in measure, it must also justify, even with the bleak logic of despair.

But Christians are men of hope. And their hope exists and is strong and has its own mysterious logic. And this remains so—but not because Christ has died. (Indeed, if that were all, we would require no one to tell us that our faith is vain.) Rather, our hope is in the One who has undergone death on our behalf and has mysteriously and marvelously risen.

Yet the modern death image of the Savior, so often static, speechless, and merely human, is almost directly dissociated from the realities offered us in the New Testament, especially by St. Paul and St. John. And such an image can perform a further disservice. It can serve as a powerful excuse for believers to bow out of the hard realities of their own time and place. Being no more than a figure of human death, the image cannot help them see the truth that lies both within and beyond their own experience. It has no power, that is, to remind men that the death of Christ is past, that His death was canceled by the intervention of God in corporal resurrection.

And if believers center Christian life solely around a death image, they miss the resolution of the enigma of human suffering offered by the Passion of Christ. They miss also the radiant, virile implications present in His resurrected presence for their own time and place. Indeed,

if the religious image succeeds only in burying believers
in a past event, religion itself may even induce a kind of
indifference or even a positive hostility to one's own
times—those times in which the risen Christ continues, age
on age, His mysterious and painful work of cosmic unity.

The death image we speak of is also dissociated in
principle form the community. It tends, rather, to favor
individual and subjective emotion. And when this individ-
ualism, rugged and soft at once, comes before the public
life of man, it can tend to ignore the summons of Christian
action. It can bear with injustice, poverty, segregation, the
defacement of the image of Christ in the human family.
And it can even dignify this coldness of heart with the
name Christian detachment. It tends to live in the community of men under a sense of mental shrinking and
duress, as though the Christian vocation to mankind were
a punishment or a penance. From such lives, indeed, the
"faulty excellence" of the human is all but erased. Instead
one notes a denatured, hyperangelic sense of life, entirely
at the mercy of fear and reaction.

This image is dissociated, finally, from life itself, as
death is by definition. St. Paul had spoken abruptly of the
crucial importance of the victory of Christ to the spirituality of the Christian. "If Christ has not risen," he said, "vain
then is our preaching, vain too is your faith" (1 Cor
15:14). One is compelled to wonder whether Christ has
risen over many Christian lives of today. For faith without
a sense of victory is almost literally a faith without hope. It
is myopic and defeatist. It is deprived of that tranquil
historical sense that can glance backward without a coward's longing and forward without fear. So deprived, it
can never hope to sense the marvelous shape that Providence confers on man's life. Protesting and unhappy, such
faith is the merest human endurance.

But sacred art, if it is true to reality, grants man an entrance both into faith and into human life. And it assures him that if he has the courage to accept the shape of reality, he will know a victory. "Jesus is Lord" (1 Cor. 12:3). The death and resurrection of the Savior have created that measure of light which man's heart must know if he is not to fall into inertia and discouragement.

But Christian life, his art reminds the believer, is no less exigent for being assured its victory. It tests the fiber of man to the uttermost. It exposes him to the anguish of decision, the immanence of failure. But like the art that nourishes it, this life is assured of one incalculable advantage: it lives in the real world, it has grasped things as they are.

6. Notes on Renewal

THE IRONIES OF God are strange indeed. And one of the most striking of them all is the fact that those countries which are meeting with the harshest kind of cultural and political upheaval are at present giving the Church her best leads on renewal. Without oversimplifying things, it remains true that Latin America, Africa, and Europe, each afflicted in one way or another by the travail of world change, have offered the most radical and imaginative insights into the nature of change and its applications to the tasks before us. The point is an instructive one. Rates of Church growth or the wealth and smooth operation of structures are not the decisive factors in Church vitality. Nor does deeply relevant thought always, or even usually, proceed from normal times; awakening seems rather to recur when men are hard put, when the times offer only harsh or unpromising conditions to the Church.

Such a state of things is strictly providential and deeply hopeful as well. What really counts in the Church, as the world has come to realize anew since Pope John, is the courage, inventiveness, and sacred trust that she is able to place in the breach of human life. And we must never underestimate the part that suffering and crisis play in renewing life forces. Would we have had, for instance, such moving interventions on behalf of a Church of poverty from the Latin-American bishops if the Church there had not already tasted the bitter experience of poverty and the scandalous exploitation of the poor?

When we come to apply such reflections to ourselves, we have good leads on the general sources of the renewal we seek. For it is a law of life that a living being cannot renew itself in a vacuum. One must first taste and reflect on life as it is actually occurring around and within him. He must submit to its unpredictability without becoming a victim of despair, a cynic, or a defeatist. He must come to a respect for change and must understand its nature in order to become an artisan of meaningful change. All this requires a courage of the highest order. No one has a blueprint of the forms that the life of Christians ought to take as our century goes forward; to presume so would be a ludicrous error. It was the error, in fact, of those imagined, before Vatican Council II got under way, that the Church could come to a new sense of things merely by adjusting matters of discipline or by tightening the ties of the local churches with Rome. The real task was something far different; it lay beyond the powers of all but the most courageous and clairvoyant. And we are still witnessing the struggle that the task of renewal implies. It is a struggle, in fact, of which the Council could be called only the first act.

Meantime, it is good to reflect that the very existence of the Christian is bound up with the well-being of his brothers. The Church is discovering this anew, so the statement will perhaps be a good starting point on a discussion of personal and community renewal.

Awakening to the supreme value of relationships is indeed not only a sign of adulthood; it also marks the presence of psychic health. It is, finally, a sign of the presence of the Spirit. The awakened Christian has come to see his brothers as something infinitely more than a neutral aggregate of "the others." Were such the case, the Christian would stand with the blind man of Mark's Gospel who saw "men as though they were trees, but walking about." Such eyes are still unhealed; they are not capable of judging reality. A further healing is absolutely necessary before such a man can stand within the seeing community and take up life with an awakened conscience. Until man is healed with the healing of Christ, he is congenitally unable to discern his brethren, to judge their need and respond to it. At the same time, he cannot hope to know himself with any measure of accuracy—not, that is, as a mere object among others, but as a center of community, one who stands within a network of viable consciences, mutually responsible, mutually responding.

For the awakened man, the universe has meaning, density, and value precisely because the "others" are not merely *there* but *here*, are within him. His conscience is a spiritual enclosure large enough to contain, generous enough to bear with, strong enough to give order to, the bewildering forms of hope, fear, transgression, and ignorance as well as of moral courage and grandeur that are the forms of modern life itself.

This Christian consciousness is not a sheepfold. Nor is it ruled over by an owner of sheep. The point is perhaps worth stressing, if only because the temptation of massive "doing good," of sheep dipping, inoculating, and shearing, can diminish our understanding of others, their freedom in approaching us, and our freedom in welcoming them. Something much more radical and difficult than mere doing good is asked of us by the gospel. Rather than casting a man outside himself, the gospel begins by probing the quality of personal lives. Man, the Lord implies, becomes worthy of life, worthy of responsibility, when he submits to inner change.

The gospel outlines a catechumenate of the Spirit, designed to form human beings according to the hope of Christ. In the tradition of St. John, the transcendent character of conversion is stressed. Man must be reborn of water and the Holy Spirit. Or, in a related dramatic symbol, he is instructed to go and wash, and he returns seeing. Further, he must eat the bread of life if he is to have life in him. It is finally God's gift that works the deepest human change; God alone can create and re-create. "No one can come to me unless the Father . . . draw him" (Jn. 6:44).

But John's insistence on mystery is in no case an automation that degrades the human response to God's invitation. Indeed, our theology is just beginning to recover a sense of the sublime respect for human life implied in the religion of John. The initiative in man's awakening to Christ is always on the part of God, but it implies a free act of submission by man; and every further gift of God awaits in man a measure of holy awareness, maturity, and susceptibility to grace. John, insisting on God's grandeur, still knows what is in man. Speaking of the disciples, he conveys a sense of the tentativeness of their first steps toward the Savior, of their human reservations and puerile hopes, and then the growth in freedom, wisdom, and courage as these men, standing uneasily on the edge of the Savior's circle, are slowly led to the center of crisis and decision, to their part in Christ's death and victory, and to consequent responsibility.

The tradition of Luke is in a sense gentler, more humane and immanent. It stresses man's activity in being saved. Often, Luke identifies conversion with discipleship. A man is invited to stand at Christ's side, by an act that disclaims his former life in favor of a new sense of the other. "Sell all that thou hast . . . and come, follow me." "If anyone wishes to come after me, let him . . . take up his cross." "Follow me. . . . Let the dead bury their dead." In such a view of life, the past is stripped away, not only of its passion for childish possessions, but also of the pagan instinct, subtly

alive even in the converted, to use the name of the Rabb
in the service of human pride. To combat this, Luke
places conversion almost invariably under the sign of the
cross. "Can you drink of the cup of which I drink?"

Whether one speaks of the tradition of John or of Luke
a single impression abides. Human change invariably oc
curs through the agency of persons. Other species of
change, worked by influences more or less impersonal (our
century has multiplied these forms to an almost unbear
able degree), are invariably frivolous or destructive. The
point is worth dwelling on, not only because talk of change
and analysis of change are so much in the air today. More
nearly to our point is the fact that personal change, and
the kind of social change that loses none of its personal
ism, is a law of life itself. The Incarnation did not except
itself from this law. God in Christ has placed at the heart
of existence change of a very special kind; not any change
at all, not an automatic or magical or unconscious *mystique*
of nature or grace. Christ introduces a new possibility into
human history, a new energy of love and intelligence that
will enable man to grasp reality with assurance and wis
dom. His gift to us is a power that is both intuitive and
synoptic; it introduces us to the inner features of life and
enables us to hold before our gaze the truth of things, with
all its implications and relationships. And finally, He en
ables us to choose without being blinded by passion or
childishness.

The change to which Christ invites us is in fact a re
covery of, or a strengthening of, the sense of the person
New directions often have their finest value precisely in
this. Underlying the sense of unrest with old ways of
thought, with outworn language, predictable reactions
climates of life that are imported or stale or false, is some
thing extremely precious. The person is coming through

once more. He may have felt himself duped or trapped; he may have sensed that a given atmosphere was forbidding him to be himself. Or he could not accept the terms under which life was presented; they seemed to him arbitrary or childish or sterile. And if he is fortunate, he breaks through; and in breaking through, not with desperation or clumsy or wounding acts, but with the quiet determination of the Spirit, he finds that communion is possible with others too. Those others, perhaps engaged in the same ideal and pursuing the same form of life, had seemed to form a ring of silence around him. And how strange it is, he thinks, that silence should have prevailed so long, that mere politeness and a sense of amenities should have prevented each from touching the heart and hope of the other.

The greatest changes within human life thus come to pass when a man has awakened to the existence of his brethren. And when we come to think of our own times, we must take heart that such an awakening is actually occurring all around us, in the most unexpected places and in lives one would have placed least hope in. What a momentous thing it is that Christians who are willing to spend themselves for their brethren need never stand alone. There are always others ready to stand with us; altruism cuts across all lines of dogma and culture, allowing a brother to meet a brother's hand across the human need one is determined to serve.

Christians are sometimes tempted to lose a measure of their potential in trying to conserve their identity too closely. They forget, or they fear, to take chances on others. They become so obsessed with organization and stability that they lose present opportunities of service. They insist that a given work must be saluted as Christian; meantime, the work itself risks being neglected or left to others or badly or thoughtlessly done. Whereas the real point is

surely that any work at all affecting the moral life of man
or bringing hope to his human condition deserves the
name Christian and will bear fruit in the hour of God.

Indeed, the point of preserving Christian identity is less
a matter of tightening the lines of Church institutions or
marking them clearly off from other structures than it is a
matter of casting Christians "into the deep." It is in a
rigorous attachment to the will of Christ that we are to
find ourselves. And such effort will embrace all men, all
cultures, all human efforts. It implies a dynamic of redemption that is less concerned with fears, preservation, and
institutions than with world need and world service. How
otherwise indeed than by such an effort of understanding
love does an adult come to self-awareness? In an adult life,
a sense of actual life invades the person, cleanses his
personality of all residual self-love, smallness of heart,
egoism, idolatry of the past, childish dreams, and sets up
in their place world resonances that cast the center of
one's existence upon the wild sea of the world. Far from
losing himself there, the Christian glories in the truth that
he has truly found himself, in the depth and height and
breadth of that charity with which Christ has filled the
universe.

A period of suffering, perhaps very extended and bitter,
seems almost inevitably to precede and accompany the
kind of change we are speaking of. In the nature of things,
no one comes easily or automatically to a new stage of
adulthood. The past and the present are always safe
ground; they represent the known, the tried and true; and
precisely in that measure, they offer the greatest temptation to remain on terra firma, to make little sorties into
one's immediate surroundings, but to insist more or less
consciously that the present is the measure of the future.
Such tactics can hardly be called the material of true hu-

man or social change; they may add inches to one's gains, but what is really in question is the universalism of Christ, the cosmic vocation of the Word Incarnate, living on in men of daring and imagination and the capacity for great hope.

In speaking in this way, one is not, of course, recommending a kind of romanticism that costs nothing and achieves nothing. There is always a temptation to dream away valuable time, to indulge in fruitless and ambiguous hope of "conquest," to embrace an illusion of success. But adulthood is something else again. A hard and costly discipline is always implied if one is to arrive at a sense of the value of past experience so that what has been gained at great cost is not lost in the hope of coming to something better, something more realistic and authentic.

Perhaps one criterion that will help us separate mere dreams from acts of purposeful love is that of Incarnation, as Gabriel Marcel suggests. In any serious question of renewal, we are asked to go deeply in two concrete directions, both of them real, both mysterious. These directions are the mystery of the world and the mystery of Christ; and we are asked to find the unitive link that connects the two directions. Such an effort—taken step by step, with respect for the hope and ideas of those around us, proceeding with simplicity, direct speech, and a sense of the hopes that are laid up in us by Christ and by His world— anchors our hope in discipline, respect for community, and patience.

The mystery of the world is the mystery of Christ. The Pauline vision of life first opened before the eyes of Christians this staggering proportion of reality. Apart from Paul, the temptation of the early communities (and, indeed, our own temptation) would be a continuing, more or less unconscious effort to attain clarity by way of diminution, to construct for our own comfort a Cartesian Christ whose reality could be grasped and held in a concept, a Christ who was apart from process and time, apart from civilizations and social upheaval, ignorant of the massive, cosmic providence speaking to us from within time and this world.

The thought of Paul offers a corrective here. Though he was the visionary of Christ's transcendence, he was also impregnated with a sense of the divine immanence and presence. Christ was a God of glory, risen, triumphant, standing at the end of things, unable to be touched by pain or anguish or the tides of malice. But at the same time, "we are the completion of Him who is everywhere complete." We are "His manhood," "His Body." In us, God takes the world seriously—not merely in a historical action, once accomplished and done with, but in continuing sacramental activity, in the social consequence of personal conversion to Him, in drawing men to His side by free choices, in the progressive efforts to master the universe, to achieve dignity, stability, and hope in the human community. Of all these efforts, Christ is the end; He gives them inner coherence and direction. In His victory He draws men irresistibly toward Himself, guaranteeing that His Church will never become a victim of time and this world, that she will never lose her essential transcendence, her power of purifying and elevating hope beyond the terrain of this world. He "draws us to the Father."

But if the end is transcendent and assured, the way is also holy. It is also, as any adult can tell today, bitter, without apparent issue, ringed round with fires of despair and human insolvency and malice. It is crucial, therefore, that the One who stands at the end of things takes His stand not as mere spectator or even as One who confers a generalized approval or encouragement on those who come forward, bloodied in the conflict. The Victor must take the struggle seriously. And to do this, He must in a sense still stand within the struggle.

It is in order to assure for Himself an authentic, human, tried existence, a life in the breach, that Christ has created us, His own Body. In us, He continues to take the world seriously. In us, His consciousness takes flesh once more, a tactile, visible presence of intelligence, hope, effort, compassion. In us, His will to save all, to bind up and heal and renew, has local habitation.

What this can mean for the world, for that unkillable residue of hope that lies within the consciousness of good men everywhere, we are just beginning to realize anew. The realization is, in a sense, a prime ingredient of our renewal. It is supremely necessary that the world's hope for us, unformulated, mute, generalized, and unpurified though it be, have shape and scope within our own hearts. If we renew ourselves, it is at once for the honor of Christ and for the hopes of the world that are at present so near despair as almost to be unrecognizable. But these hopes, to speak positively, are at times heroic and have an astonishing power of renewing our own hopes as well. What does the world expect of the Church? The question is humiliating in the extreme, as the imbroglio over *The Deputy* has shown us. The world hopes, in fine, that our own capacities for clarity of conscience, for the inward reading of history, and for breadth of judgment will surpass the moral vision which the world itself is able to offer in times of crisis. In the moral order, the world hopes for more of the Church than it does of itself.

Today men are only slowly becoming convinced that we do take them seriously, that we are able to offer them from within world experience a moral leadership of a pure and prophetic order. The Vatican Council has helped in crystallizing this hope, and so has the miraculous work of

Pope John. But one can still think soberly of enormous moral dilemmas on which the Church has not yet exerted her influence, where caution and prudence still tend to rule everything. We hope with all our hearts that the serious treatment accorded to Schema 13 by the Fathers of the Council in its fourth session will turn the tide—for the Church and the world alike. Nuclear warfare, population explosion, world poverty, adaptation of missionary efforts, conversation with men of all faiths, a new openness with Marxists, worldwide racial conflicts—these are a few of the moral questions that must shortly win an unequivocal response from the Church.

At this point, it will perhaps bear stressing once more that taking the world seriously, in the sense we speak of, is a way of taking Christ seriously. Studying the Church during these periods when her witness was purest and most winning, we find that she hardly knew any other way. Or rather let us say that her sacramental and verbal activity moved in the direction of concrete world service. She was a community of incarnate consciences, which stretched themselves to the limits of the moral universe in an all embracing act of love and restoration. And in including all lives, the Church included all moral dilemmas; not precisely in order to solve them, since she also walked in a kind of darkness. Rather, she shed upon them warmth of Christ's wisdom, compassion, and presence. Simply, she stayed with human life. Often she could do no more than bring men a measure of hope, but she knew that this was indeed a very great thing. She stood with those whose lives seemed to be a long series of human impasses—the rejected, the poor, the segregated. And so she must stand today, in the multiple crises that technology, troubled peace, and the uneven human development of the world are bringing men. In any of these circumstances, her character is vindicated anew—friend of man, a moral presence that relieves men of the slavery of blind anguish and despair.

Such fidelity to the human condition works a great change within the Church also. It purifies her of the temptation of grandeur and legalism. In such a way, the world is seen as a form of the Providence of Christ for the Church also. Modesty, concrete effort, simplicity of style of life, clairvoyance, good sense—these are the qualities of a renewal that has taken its start not from an ideal Church or an ideal world but from the truth of things: a living Christ in a real world.

It would be posing things falsely and setting up impossible dilemmas to put the question of renewal merely in terms of problems and solutions, whether we are speaking of individual lives, of communities, or of the world itself. This kind of abstraction is at best questionable and at worst destructive. The real point of renewal is something very different, an inventive love that enables us to draw closer to one another to discover points of greatest need in our world—needs that can be met here and now with the energies available to us. This, together with a continuing openness of mind and heart that helps us to meet change within or around us with a measure of suppleness and courage, is central to renewal.

Again, there is an enormous difference between renewal and mere restoration. One can always restore Gothic architecture or plainchant and conclude that he has achieved something of value. But such work is taxidermic rather than creative. And it finally serves only to comfort the pusillanimous. An infinitely more demanding task is asked of those who seek renewal; it includes searching out essentials, listening and learning from the living, having the prophetic courage to "root out and pull down" as the preliminary to new life.

And in such a process, it will bear saying once more, the

real world keeps getting in. Men and women who live in
the modern world by choice do not come to decisions with
the world put safely to one side, as though, indeed, one
could announce the direction and meaning of modern life
without having paid the price of sympathy and commu
nion. In any true renewal, the world must be served, its
voice heard; otherwise, we risk offering no more than
another ecclesiastical solution to a worldly problem, some
thing beside the mark, something that has not paid the
price of living in and for the world—an answering voice
which therefore is radically incapable of speaking on the
world's behalf.

To speak on behalf of the world, to be determined to
serve the world, to identify with its struggle and hope
does not erase the difference between that world and our
selves. Such a loss of identity of principle occurs, paradoxi
cally enough, not when men are giving themselves to
others, but when they are hoarding human life, for even
the most sacred reasons. The question of what constitutes
living faith would lead us too far afield here. But one can
at least suggest in passing that if the act of faith is seen
concretely as a gift of God in Christ, inviting us to sonship
of the Father in a community of brothers, to an adventure
of love that will have no end, then love of our brethren, as
well as responsibility toward them, is the very ground of
our life in God.

Such a sense of faith frees it of all arrogance and exclu
siveness. If faith implies a difference between Christians
and nonbelievers, and indeed it does, the difference is best
seen from the point of view of the invitation of God, of an
undeserved gift that is mysteriously offered to all men. For
those who are summoned to membership in the commu
nity where grace is not merely present but "abounds,"
responsibility is, of course, greater. Christians, in the na

ture of things, are called to a deeper understanding, a greater capacity for service, intelligence, and love.

Of course, the difference, the mystery that we call Christian, becomes visible in a style of life, in a formed and illumined conscience. But it is particularly striking today that the outlines of our style of life, when they are very pure and open, coincide more and more with the consciences, the aspirations, and qualities of other lives. The fact can be very disturbing in its first shock. There is a mysterious development of conscience taking place in the world, and this development parallels many new aspects of conscience within the Church. It sometimes goes even further, exerting a positive pressure on Christians to take up unpopular causes, to exercise a purer, more courageous presence.

Such reflections lead one to suggest that faith in Christ is attractive to others today not in terms of enclosure and outer world so much as in a mysterious interpenetration of grace that summons a brother to the side of his brother and finds that differences are given a new perspective in mutual service.

Thus the effort toward renewal is not self-centered but relational. The renewal we seek for ourselves is to be found most surely in the strength of the human relationships we are able to create and sustain with others. Our method, our *mystique*, as Péguy called it, is to incarnate relationships, to ground ourselves firmly in other lives, to give visible form to the mystery of Christ's brotherhood and, in the process, to extend the mystery itself, to make it apparent, palatable, attractive.

In speaking of renewal in terms of relationships, we are obviously not recommending religious homogenization. Neither are we defending an aping of modern mores that merely turns the Church into a comfort station for the worldly. Nor are we commending the fantasy that presumes that the world will listen to us only if we consent to become less markedly Christian. Paul's insistence on the cross in his Letter to the Christians of Corinth remains of the essence, for then as for now. Still, two points occur as relevant here. The violence of Paul's attack on the wisdom of the Greek world and his fierce words on the paradox of the cross must be balanced by another emphasis. In his great speeches in the Acts, he is evidently searching out points of concordance, areas of mutual love and intellectual sympathy. The cross of Christians obviously is not to be identified with whatever is new or unfamiliar in the pagan world.

To speak more nearly of ourselves, it is important that the form which the cross of Christ takes in our own era be accurately understood. Christians in the past have sometimes shouldered a cross that they piously imagined was of the world's fashioning. But if its lineaments were clearly seen, such a cross was merely the outward form of their own fear and cowardice.

Love of others, manful effort of service, the will to enter and understand lives different from our own lives—such are at least a few of the forms of the evangelical cross. Such suffering is a way of growth and understanding rather than of restrictive complacence; it is also deeply humbling. The Christians who are carrying the burden of love for others are continually encountering men and women, perhaps deprived of explicit faith in Christ, who themselves are bearing great burdens of responsibility and love of the world. For encounters with such men, we Christians can only be grateful; they free us of the obsession that we alone carry the world's burdens, that we alone understand Christ, or that, in biblical terms, we "possess God." A genuine apostolic sense is the surest guarantee against such idolatry.

Genuine renewal, in contrast to all efforts at false purity, isolationism, and spiritual selfishness, places us more deeply in the soil that sustains and invigorates the living. That soil is the word of God and the sacramental acts of Christ, both of these verified and made present in history, in this world. The soil is, in short, the immensely rich mold of God's gifts of nature and grace in which every community must be nurtured. To uproot oneself from this soil is, in the nature of things, to court death. History is the best teacher of this. Whenever the living flower of the Church was uprooted in order to place its future in the soil of sacristy or of sanctuary, it withered away. It became a decoration of life instead of an essential growth within life. It lost the power to bear fruit; it could no longer sustain and refresh living men. Neither could it bear the harsh tempestuous climate of real life. It became a hot house growth for special souls; it was condemned to politeness, a religion of occasion and formalism.

These reflections can perhaps be given more practical point by the questions and comments that follow:

1. Are laymen determined to be fully lay in (*a*) understanding and (*b*) style of life?

(*a*) *Understanding.* There are two poles here: baptism and a world of laicity. Baptism consecrates our relationships to the world, to matter, to social and personal change, to community. The world, in an ever more determined and skillful control of nature, exerts an opposite, balancing pressure on the sacramental mystery. It welcomes men who respect the world—not merely as "secondary cause" but as value. Even in dogmatic extremes of secularism, the world's attempt at self-understanding can illumine our problem—how to love the world, the indispensable condition of membership in a world community; how to lead beyond by being truly within; how to judge by way of understanding. And, conversely, the problem is how to

give substance and visibility to a Church that is peren-
nially tempted to veer off into Platonism, to avoid the task
of serving and respecting, to condemn involvement, to
misread the meaning of the "one thing necessary." To be
lay, then, is (at least tentatively) to be in the world by
communion of value, communication of truth, critique of
progress. It is serving the world by *being* the Church
rather than serving the Church by being *in* the Church.

(b) *Style of life.* The difficulty with lay communities is
that no recent or even remote period of the Church has
offered a lead on their development under the double sign
of sacrament and world. Modern lay communities were
forced, in the nature of things, to draw on the experience
of religious communities. It was predictable that such
realities as poverty, chastity, obedience, authority, methods of prayer, and choice of apostolates would influence
lay communities, with more or less accidental modifica-
tion. The time has pershps come for a new look at the
bases of lay community life, especially in light of the
mobility of social life in the world and the forces that draw
men together in team enterprises, research, service abroad.
One finds in such groups a strong sense of fraternity,
friendship, spontaneity, as well as special competence, international sense, humaneness, capacity for adaptation,
cultural openness.

It is not at all clear *a priori* that the religious counsels
should shape the pattern of lay Catholic groups that en-
vision a lifetime commitment. Neither is it certain that the
secular institutes represent a successful pattern of adaptation.

2. Are we able to distinguish cultural Catholicism from
universal Catholicism?

The former is almost inevitably and invariably helpless
once it is off the home ground; it is out of its depth in the
world at large. And the question is not merely one of

personal alienation from what is unexpected or assaulting. There is the more serious difficulty of inability to communicate, to evaluate, to share and contribute. If the "cultural" Catholic goes abroad, he becomes a thoughtless importer of his cultural baggage or the uneasy critic of local mores or the last of the colonials. The idea that the orders of humanism, creation, and redemption form a temporal and spatial unity everywhere in the world is foreign to such a one. So he remains a foreigner to all incarnations of humanism, creativity, or redemption that are not in his hometown handbook. The handbook is nothing so mysterious or exigent as the gospels or a sense of the mystery of man. It is, rather, a scrapbook of local mores and morals, of national folklore, of ways of thought that have cut Christ and man down to manipulable size.

Universal Catholicism dwells both in inspired documents and in universal man. The latter is, of course, our point here. Such men are obviously not Catholics without culture. But their culture is untainted by nationalism; it is neither overrefined nor static nor defensive. It is a living edge of mind, honed in experience and reflection, ready for encounter with other minds, able to cut across the accretions of the past, the unexamined myth. It is a source of communion; having touched the sources of man's existence in its own inquiry, it is able to grasp both what is irreducible in man's existence and what is still open, unachieved, and possible in his future.

3. What of institutions and persons and their relative importance?

The point here is a fresh look at institutions as they face a changing world and a changing Church. No one of them can be called *ipso facto* valuable; their nature is that of service and tool, and as such they are subject to constant revaluation.

The first question is always that of pneumatic communities, incarnate consciences that may or may not choose to create structures as their instrument of service. Putting persons ahead of things is the first method of freedom; it readies us for crisis, loss, and change, since it finds us literally "having nothing." The relationship of structures to persons is admittedly a delicate one. It will bear saying, though, that modern men long for the symbolic activity of unprotected people, whose poverty of spirit is a source of healthy shock in affluent societies and gains an immediate rapport with developing peoples.

4. How does ecumenism touch our question of renewal? The question at first glance seems an easy one; we answer it by continuing to encourage friendships and discussions and hospitality. Such an answer reflects a general assumption: a core of formed Roman Catholics is to be the primary apostolic influence of the Church on the world of man. So easy an answer ought to make thinking men uneasy. And for two principal reasons: (a) the Council has been careful and delicate in formulating a definition of the Church that would include all the baptized; and (b) the Council, in its hesitations and delays, has been a learner before the world. It is also true that many lay groups that begin in theory to serve and mediate between Church and world end up serving ecclesiastical institutions or themselves becoming another institution of the Church. Instead of taking their stand on the frontier, they edge progressively closer to the center.

A tentative question might be: what sources of life are open to lay groups from *without*? Are there not new steps to be taken so that the *sancta unitas* may be symbolized more powerfully by those whose Christian sense is also deeply secular, who see the tasks of the common good as a powerful unitive force for consciences of differing traditions? Perhaps Protestants and Catholics would discover a

real unity more quickly by an act of faith *in the world?*
And, conversely, does not a rigorous Christianity, a mélange
of unexamined elements—faith, culture, the past—tend
inevitably to an ever-constricting circle, an exclusive faith
in contrast to an inclusive one?

5. A related question: do present forms of lay life inhibit
or encourage social conscience?

The question is a difficult one; the answer is bound to be
tentative. But the discussion may be encouraged by this
reflection: in a given society there are usually no more
than three or four really crucial social problems in the air.
To define them, to act on them is the task of any lay group
worthy of existing at all. To miss their point, on the other
hand, or to temporize in their regard is literally to lose
everything.

6. What is the function of liturgy in lay groups?

The question, again, is a very large one. Liturgy, as
meant here, and following on Pius XII, is the determining form of both our life in God and our attitudes toward
the human scene. Liturgical activity that does not take
the second of these into account is self-defeating. (It
must be apparent that the second of these has up to the
present been largely neglected.) We have presumed that
the actions of Christ will automatically become models of
our actions without interpretation or insistence.

But liturgy properly understood helps lay groups understand not only their sacred dignity but their laicity as
well—not Christ alone or apart, but Christ in His world;
not the community alone or apart, but the community in
and of the world.

The community at worship is by definition a penetration of sacred space by secular presence; and liturgical
activity leads, according to the intention of Christ, to the
penetration of secular space (the world) by sacred pres-

ence (Christian conscience in action). But, in fact, this happens infrequently. And it practically never happens when the voice from the pulpit (or its equivalent) is silent.

7. Are laymen not invited to review their relationship to Church authority as a part of their own renewal?

It would seem so. Just as the Church is slowly undertaking an examination in depth of the meaning of authority and is coming to something much more humane and supple, so we are invited to move in the same direction. Collegiality, in other words, ought not to stop with the bishops. Just as the Council witnessed a kind of sacred "declaration of independence" from excesses of centralism and bureaucracy, so the layman is invited to reconsider his own obedience as a way to a new relationship with the authority of the Church. It is perhaps worth noting here that for a Christian, as for any man, independence is never an end in itself; it has value insofar as it clears the ground for new, fresh, vital relationships. Thus collegiality, properly understood, does not merely mean independence from this or that. It implies new relationships, new initiatives, and a newly realized service, along with new possibilities of discharging that service, with respect for local needs and hopes. Is it not to be thought that the laymen, closer geographically and sacramentally to many of the springs of modern life, would gain by reviewing his understanding of authority in light of his insights, his fears and hopes, his stake in the life of man? In specifically lay tasks, the layman is to be respected and heard. Where necessary, he must insist on being respected and heard.

The tasks we have in mind take the layman not only within the world as presence but toward action on behalf of the world. There would ideally be no conflict between consciences that integrate a passion for human justice and consciences that bear specific authority from Christ in His Church. The second type of conscience ideally includes the first, at least in a generalized way. But where conflicts do exist, it is a function of lay integrity to make the terms of the conflict clear, to seek its resolution, not by taking the easy way out, in submission, but by way of clear speech and needful action, by dialogue, by courage. One is not talking in the abstract here; problems such as racial conflicts, nuclear armaments, and crises of conscience do not wait on irrelevancies. They demand men who can act clear-sightedly, competently, without delays over permissions that have already been granted and powers that have already been conferred—in baptism and confirmation.

7. St. Paul: Figure of Crisis

THE PRESENT CHAPTER will deal with realities which from the historical point of view are profoundly related. A period of crisis, as we shall suggest, forged the liturgy of the Western Church. And this liturgy, as its greatest achievement, formed men of crisis in the Church who were endowed with a new world view and an acute social conscience.

It seems verifiable that many influences—background, new faith, religious community—conspired to make the early Christians men of crisis. In the first place, the central event of their faith had been the supreme crisis in religious history. The Son of God, in becoming man, in dying and rising, had introduced an altogether unforeseen element into the world and had brought about a new creation (2 Cor. 5:17), in which believers were confronted with ineluctable choices. These choices rested upon the nature of time and eternity, the meaning of man, human destiny—in fact, upon all the questions that man has regarded from time immemorial as the irreducible questions of life, the posing of which is a way of wisdom.

When a Christian placed the questions anew, it is true that he had his answers at hand; but it is profoundly false to conclude that the answers were given him by way of foreclosure of the mind. Rather, the intellectual and moral insights that came to him through the Incarnation were a way of inducing further crisis, a series of risks that were

[124]

inevitable once man entered on the Christian "way" (Acts 16:18). A man did not come to Christianity during those centuries by way of infancy or of adult neutrality. He came with the gifts and judgment of what St. Paul calls the natural man (Eph. 2:3). It was a term that, given the times, implied an extremely rich human content of Jewish or Greek genius, a passionate, activist cast of mind that knew its own "way" and pursued it with a fierce energy and purpose.

If we view the early Church in the light of such converts, whose writings give us a glimpse of their mind, it is clear that they had determined to leave behind them at the baptistry none of the world-shaping unrest that had constituted the genius of their former communities. In those communities, Jewish or pagan, the men of leadership were men of crisis. It was by way of a shattering personal crisis that they had come to the faith. And it was clear that they would see Christianity in the same terms—as a faith likely to induce crisis at the core of existence and to enable man to stand firm under the consequences that the faith both announced and set in motion.

Historical crisis was in no sense a Christian innovation. It had been an important clue to the greatness of pre-Christian pagans. And among these, the Greek dramatic heroes might be taken as ideal images of men who saw life as a passage into greater awareness of man and his world— a passage constantly beset, stimulated, and urged forward by crises of every kind. The dramatic hero represented all men in the process man must undergo as the price of remaining human. And this process, as the tragedies unfolded it, was the very opposite of human stasis or unawakened consciousness. Human life was rather an agon, a dolorous conflict in whose course man confronted life and its forces, released upon him by the god of life. According

to this view, suffering was indispensable in human formation. "To learn is to suffer" was the laconic Greek formula.
Man came to understand that only through the fury and
tempest of moral anguish would he arrive at wisdom. And
the struggle itself, as a prelude to submission, resolution,
and synthesis, was holy; it was the will of the gods.

It would not be an exaggeration to say that it was under
the image of tragic man that mankind came of age. The
Greek hero, in this sense, is a worthy symbol of mankind.
He stood purified of the forces of revolt and arrogance. He
had learned in the fires of sorrow the truth that love of the
gods and man was no slavish expedient but, rather, the
acceptance of the burden and glory of human life. The
struggle of the Greek hero, then, had elements that were
both deeply personal and inescapably social. It implied
the will to be present to others; not only the gods but the
community stood at his side, witness, judge, and compas-
sionate advocate.

One thinks in this regard of the plague scenes of
Oedipus, in which death streams outward from the king's
throne and inundates the city, a symbol of the endemic,
unexamined evil in the king's heart. A single illness chal-
lenges the energies of king and community; and the king
summons the people to join him in resolving the ugly
enigma in which all are caught. "Come, listen to me; act
as the crisis demands, and you shall have relief from all
these evils."

One thinks too of the citizens' chorus in Sophoclean
tragedy passing moral judgment on the protagonist:

> Haughtiness and the high hand of disdain
> tempt and outrage God's holy law;
> And any mortal who dares hold
> no immortal Power in awe
> will be caught up in a net of pain,

the price for which his levity is sold.
Let each man take due warnings, then,
and keep his hands from holy things.

In *Antigone* the crisis takes the form of strife between
law and personalism, announced by Creon. It is resolved
finally by risk and reasonableness, and the crisis brings to
its heights the moral greatness of the heroine. Antigone
speaks to the king:

Your edict, King, was strong
but all your strength is weakness against
the immortal unrecorded laws of God. . . .
This death of mine
is of no importance; but if I had left my brother
lying in death unburied, I should have suffered.
Now I do not.

Greek tragedy, then, brings us nearer an understanding
of those generalized and powerful moral forces which were
gathering strength in Western paganism, awaiting the
moment of Christian intervention. Providence could
scarcely have found on the Buddhist scene or the Hindu
scene human presuppositions that were from so many
points of view indispensable to the birth of a Christian
mind in man.

In the Eastern religions, the hero, if one can use the
term at all, was simply a captive of the gods. His human
endowments, the power of knowledge and of love, were a
tranquil vessel formed to contain the divine will. Man
ascended to the divine in a deliberately cultivated passivity. There was no other way to holiness; the neophyte to
the life of monk or Brahmin had to become skillful in a
formal stasis before the eternal will.

In the writings of Lao-tzu, Buddha, Mencius, and Con-
fucius, we note this effort toward an eternity open only

to those who follow a way of freedom from the world
and the community. And Western observers such as the
seventeenth-century Jesuits, Matteo Ricci, in China, and
de Nobili, in India, wrote sympathetically but critically of
these mystical tendencies, so exalted and yet so distrustful
of time and this world. One senses the reverence of the
Jesuits for a religious life that had come to such grandeur
so far in time and place from the truth of Christ. We sense
too the difficulty with which these contemplative activists
of the West, with their tradition of the absolutely crucial
nature of time, entered this Eastern world of fragile, other
worldly holiness.

The Greek and Roman worlds were something else
again. Whatever their differences of spirit, the ancient
pagan cultures commonly produced men of action who
took crisis in stride, who gloried in the intricate check and
countercheck of politics and war and religious intrigue.
They were, in fact, pragmatists whose devotion to the
tactile, visual world of man and history amounted to an
intellectual passion.

And their world was to be the world of the early Church.
In such a climate, men knew that they chose or were lost,
that history waited neither on good intentions nor on
weakness, that the mind had for its greatest task the sub
duing and synthesis of the forces of time and space, the
ingathering of men for communal willed order, beauty
law, power.

Paul and Crisis

It would be unimaginable that so firm a sense of man
and of man's world would leave the early Church unaf
fected. It affected one of the earliest converts, Paul, to the
very heart. And no wonder; he had been shaped within
the world of the Hellenistic Jew; he would continue to b

shaped by it in a hundred ways, by its subtle moral and intellectual pressures. In Paul's thought, the image that God had left of Himself in nature was nothing so simple as a landscape or a rhythm of skies and seasons. It was, rather, the moral processes of the world, made evident in pagan history—man's awakening conscience, his striving toward unity, communication, and love. It was these triumphs of paganism that Paul chose to praise in the famous discourse of the agora of Athens:

> And from one man he has created the whole human race and made them live all over the face of the earth, determining their appointed times and the boundaries of their lands; that they should seek God, and perhaps grope after him and find him, though he is not far from any one of us. For in him we live and move and have our being, as indeed some of your own poets have said, *For we are also his offspring* (Acts 17:26–28).

In Paul himself, the forces of pagan and Jewish history had met like genetic cells. In their joining, they took the shape of historical crisis. Indeed, such a man could not have been converted to Christianity in a corner. The turbulent force of his temperament had to be matched by a like violence of grace. We note in the Damascus scene (Acts 9) the shocking subjugation of the Jewish and pagan forces that dwelt in his heart—the will to power, murder, ruthless absolutism in politics and religious life; the sense that only the man of action, the man of risk, is fit to inhabit the world and able to master it. The violent Saul, who was to be the contemplative activist Paul, had to be mastered before he could rule. Into this man of crisis, who had exulted in his power to ride the whirlwind and come to its still center, a new principle of crisis was introduced.

In such a man, grace could not delay in conferring the

solaces so dear to lesser men. The conversion of Paul is a very paradigm of the essential work of Christ in man. Conversion as Paul experienced it was not designed to supply ready answers to unthinking men or a questionable unearned peace or the kind of stability that is killing to enterprise and growth. Grace had not come to tidy up the world.

And when we speak of the human effects of grace on Paul, we note how in every respect his conversion enlarged and intensified his thought. He did not become less a man in becoming Christ's man (Gal. 6:10). His view of life remained full-blooded, critical, and humane (1 Cor. 9:22). There is no hint in his Christianity of an otherworldly lassitude, an ennui before mankind, an impatience with the simple of heart (Eph. 4:2). When he reflects on his new life, Paul's every instinct moves toward a new human largeness (2 Cor. 2:15). He is able to enter other lives at their least invitation, to dwell in their dwelling, to listen and learn (1 Cor. 10:33). His mind moves quickly forward, but it leaves nothing behind; it does not seek holiness by excluding sinners (Gal. 2:17) or new knowledge by despising pagans (1 Cor. 12:13) or the good estate of the Church by destroying the synagogue (Gal. 2:15).

In this massive and living synthesis, no good thing is in conflict with any other good (Rom. 8:28, Phil. 4:8). The love of God is one with the love of man, speculation with activity, practical judgment with mystical insight. In Paul's dwelling, the Jew sits in peace with the Greek (Eph. 2:20); Paul, the Pharisee and Hellenist, will welcome and hear both (1 Cor. 9:12). And this view of life comes to its summit and center in Christ. "For all things are yours . . . and you are Christ's, and Christ is God's" (1 Cor. 3:22–23).

The inner world of Paul was transformed by his conversion, but the outer world of man remained unchanged. It remained the world of paganism and of Israel, as it had been. It had not become Christian because Paul was Christian; it went its way, it pursued its values as before. Athens received the convert Paul as though he were no more than some provincial fanatic (Acts 17:26), one among hundreds of diversions in the city square. The Jewish leadership continued, in almost every case, to resist him to the death (Acts 14:5, 17:5, 18:6, 21:28).

And Paul dealt with all this. He accepted the world as it was. He did not petulantly demand that because he had changed, the whole world should be changed. Or, rather, he saw the human implications of his apostolate. The grace of conversion was in the last analysis a gift and mystery, and no human energy or eloquence or genius could act in its stead or presume to take its place. Until the moment of God, human ingenuity or impatience was of little avail (Gal. 4:2).

A great man will always shape others to his image. It became clear in the communities rather soon after Paul's conversion that the Church would never again be as she had been. A new sense of universality was in the air. The Church advanced to the Hellenistic world, and her guide was Paul. With his conversion, indeed, the Church had won her first secure foothold in the world to which the Lord had commissioned her. In Paul, human greatness for the first time was dedicated to the service of Christ.

Indeed, when we compare Paul with the other Apostles, it is clear that almost every element of Paul's temperament contrasts strongly with that of the Twelve. He is Hellenistic, a Pharisee, a cosmopolite (Acts 26:5). The others belong to the restrictive culture of Hebraic observance. They had been summoned by the Rabbi of Galilee to an apostolate that had left them relatively undisturbed within Jewish geography and ritual (Jn. 1:39ff.). But Saul was converted at the world crossroads. The risen Lord descended like a noon thunderbolt, not so much to invite Saul to

belief as to lay hands on him in possession, the first fruits
of His irresistible victory. The Twelve had been formed
slowly over a period of years. Divine patience had entered
strongly into their pedagogy (Mt. 8:25–26). And the patience of God was manifest even as late as the Ascension
of Christ, the Apostles still remaining half-convinced and
bewildered before the world of the Spirit (Acts 1:6). But
Saul was healed and illumined in a moment. The graces
that formed the other Apostles over a long period of time
came to him instantaneously (Acts 9:4–5). So suddenly as
to bewilder the community, he was transformed from
enemy into man of the Church (Acts 9:15). And the
Church, undermanned and hard pressed, suddenly sensed
at her side one whose speech was that of friend, who bent
his efforts to her labors, who took the lead in her apostolate with astonishing energy and a holy self-forgetfulness
(Acts 9:22).

Considering the vocation of Paul, we are led to reflect
that there will never be an adequate substitute in the
Church for men whose minds are by nature large and
open, who see ecclesiastical life quite simply in terms of
human life—life elevated and blessed to be sure, but for
all that not diminished or disembodied. In the Church,
Paul was the first of such men. His faith urged him forward
to the simplest and most difficult of tasks—to examine
man's life as it took shape before him, to know and love
that life as a necessary condition of bringing it to a change
of heart. Paul brought to the faith an instinctive piety toward experience. He felt no inclination to bow out of the
chaos of his world, uninviting and even hostile as it might
appear to the word of God. He lost no time in rumination
or daydreams over the impossible good times, the ideal
human community, the hypothetical future that might be
apt to welcome the gospel. Rather, as we sense in the

letters and the account of Acts, he was marked by a respect for things as they are, for man's history and thought and sensibility. And it was through this same respect that he was granted a lucid sense of the mystery that lies at the heart of man's life—the mystery of man as a creative and redeeming force. Paul knew that man is not subject to the cycles of nature in the way that the subhuman world is. Man's dignity is precisely that he can create history by acts of intelligence and love. It is this power that allows him to transcend the inhuman cycles that in the Greek world were said to rule the fate of mankind.

By way of contrast, Paul spoke of the essentially moral and sacred structure of time. Time was task; it was the envelope of decision and new direction; it was to be redeemed. And because time was crucial, the times were brief (1 Cor. 7:29); they were weighted with the irony that redemption had brought so urgently to bear on life (2 Cor. 6:2). Man was to use creation and not to use it, to act and to submit, to enjoy and to abstain (1 Cor. 7:31). A Christian sense of time implied a sense of the heavy burdens of the community; it brought also a sense of the imminent end of things—almost at any moment, the Lord might return to announce His victory, to claim His accounting from man (1 Thess. 5:2).

In the meantime, as Paul sensed, the Christian was called to be a shaper of history. He was to make available to the community the vision of life that he had been granted. Otherwise, if he refused a protagonist's role in life, he became a recusant also before the faith. He polluted the springs of the Church's mystical life with the poison of cowardice, blighted the fruits of her sacred activity, and condemned himself to live like a parasite on "his body, the Church" (Col. 1:18).

Paul's insight arose out of his own fiery ordeal. He himself had been brought to the Church at an unpredictable hour by a crisis of grace. And his apostolate continued to make the most of time (Eph. 5:16). Such a view of life induced crisis wherever Paul went. The life of local churches took on the sharp, unmistakable features of his mind. He left neither Jewish nor Christian communities at peace, neither the laymen nor the presbyters nor the Apostles themselves, when this peace had about it the suspicion of inertia, compromise, or waste of life. And at least once, his sense of the new time inaugurated by Christ led him to a public conflict with Peter (Gal. 2:11–15).

It demands no great insight to realize that both a healthy psychology and an unusual grace were at work here. From the point of view of psychology, the adult is by definition equipped to deal with situations that inevitably arise within a community on the move. Such a community, of course, makes large demands on leadership. Its well-being requires that those in authority have a subtle and acute sense of time. Those who govern in the Church serve (Rom. 1:9, 1 Cor. 9:19). They serve by compassion and by pressure, by sensing the need of time and patience to bring men to a fuller sense of the Church. Such a sense is already presumed to exist strongly in those who hold authority. It leads them to seek out the thought of each member, conscious that the views of each will enrich the final decision.

By showing this respect, those in authority are freed from arrogance, and subjects are freed from the compulsion of being "pleasers of men" (Eph. 6:6). And the Church is freed from what is perhaps the most dangerous threat of all—the notion that decisions on matters of her practical life and action should be reached automatically, instantaneously, without criticism, debate, and exchange.

Paul's view is more human and, to a thoughtful view,

more traditionally Catholic. It implies that if the Holy Spirit guarantees to the Church correct decisions in all matters of importance, it remains true that His aid is not normally a direct intervention. It is, rather, a strengthening, enlightening, and purifying action on Christians themselves to the point where human decisions may truly reflect the divine order of things (Gal. 5:22, Eph. 5:9). In this way, the good estate of the Church is at one time a gift of eternity and a human, temporal concurrence.

A profound consciousness of the Spirit at work in all—in himself, in the community, in local leadership—marks Paul's greatness (Rom. 8:14–17). As is true of all inspired activists, there lay at the heart of the Pauline apostolate a wellspring of receptivity and openness to God (1 Cor. 2:10). It was, finally, the Spirit who guided the Church through her crises and led the Apostles by stages into a full understanding of their role (1 Cor. 2:4).

And the presence of the Spirit was in no sense equated with assurance of human success; indeed, the Paraclete showed His power in the early Church precisely on those occasions when human hopes and human pride had been silenced. At Antioch, at Athens, on the dolorous journey of captivity, in successive imprisonments, Paul tasted the bitter wine of the Spirit—invigorating and sobering, consoling and purifying (2 Cor. 1:5). He came to understand that the presence of the Holy Spirit in the Church offered little comfort to human judgment or logic. In an apparently haphazard way, Paul was bereft of comfort when it was most needed; he was left to prison, to stripes, to death (1 Cor. 4:9). He spoke with bitter resignation of the way in which the unitive action of the Spirit was sundered by false brethren (2 Cor. 11:26). He was mocked and set at naught by the powers of this world (Acts 22:24). And all the while, when his efforts seemed least to avail, he moved

forward, deeply convinced that human evidence of defeat
conceals the profound mystery of the cross and of a victory that man can neither apprehend nor bring to pass
(Rom. 6:8).

Indeed, Paul's glory is the tract on Christian hope that
he wrote to console the Christians at Rome; Paul too, like
Abraham, must hope on, refusing to substitute a debased
human hope for the fidelity of God:

> Abraham hoping against hope believed, so that he
> became the father of many nations, according to
> what was said, *So shall thy offspring be*. And with-
> out weakening in faith, he considered his own dead-
> ened body (for he was almost a hundred years old)
> . . . he did not waver through unbelief but was
> strengthened in faith, giving glory to God, being
> fully aware that whatever God has promised he is
> able to perform. Therefore it was credited to him as
> justice. Now not for his sake only was it written
> that "It was credited to him," but for the sake of us
> also, to whom it will be credited if we believe in
> him who raised Jesus our Lord from the dead, who
> was delivered up for our sins, and rose again for our
> justification (Rom. 4:18–25).

Early Liturgy and Crisis

It would seem inevitable that the strong crisis mentality
of Paul would come to affect the spirit of early Church
worship, and the supposition is, of course, historically
verifiable. In the Pauline age, Church worship was still in
formation; pioneers were infusing the liturgy of the communities with their view of life. Paul's influence on this
task becomes immediately clear when we recall that in the
local churches it was the custom to read aloud the letters
of the Apostles during the service of prayer. This service,

an extremely flexible arrangement borrowed from the Jewish synagogue, consisted of readings from Scripture, alternating with prayers and a homily.

We would rightly picture, then, at these early gatherings of the Corinthian or Philippian or Jerusalem Christians, attentive readings of the "memoirs of the apostles" (Justin). In the atmosphere of the Eucharist, an immediate and electric effect could be expected from the hearing of the word. A letter from Paul was announced. It contained the words of a man who at some previous hour had stood in the midst of the local Church giving testimony of convictions that had broken his life and reshaped it to a form of mystery and of passionate love. Now in the accents of his great heart, the presence of the Apostle was summoned once more. Here were words of reproof, of ardor, of confession, of a paternity that reached across distance and time and the chains of captivity (Col. 4:3); a voice of fatigue, a figure devoured by the privations of a heroic life; an absence that was a more spiritual presence, since he had departed from them with the "Spirit as a pledge" (2 Cor. 1:22).

The words of Paul were marked by a holy realism. They spoke of acceptance of the world, of his will to work with local conditions, to bear with the debased and brutal methods of his enemies—finally, of his will to work with man (Rom. 12:18). Simplicity and directness, patient answers to petty local difficulties, a skill in drawing minds from the most banal perplexities to the profound center of Christ (Phil. 2:1–11)—all this implied a historical fidelity of the first order. Each generation of believers, as Paul implied so often, must be marked by this sense of new life in Christ (Col. 1:18). And such fidelity to the world of man was not simply a human tactic; it implied, rather, a sense of the Church, of the fact that she must at every age take her

138   THEY CALL US DEAD MEN

stand within life. So we note in Paul's thought an atten-
tiveness to currents of man's inner life, a concern for whatever gives character and meaning to a given period, for
elements that in the truest sense form the face of man as he
seeks the truth or wanders at a distance from it.

The faith, as Paul implies, is a larger enterprise than
man will readily concede (Rom. 3:24, 4:17). It cannot be
content with forming men who are faithful only to worship, men who come to a measure of peace only by turning
their back on the world. If the Church is to be more than a
shapeless extrusion on the body of mankind, believers must
know and love their world in order to act on their world.

It became clear to Paul shortly after his conversion what
his special task in the Church was to be. He was to be
responsible for a new beginning. He was to explore life
painfully and reflectively, then to write letters to the
communities, out of the fire of circumstances, letters that
would speak of the first generation of Christians—of their
hope, their summons, their failure. He was to follow with
an attentive, paternal, gentle firmness, the course of their
response to God—to instruct, encourage, interpret, reprove.
He was to form the Church out of the raw material of
Judaism and paganism. His task was to experience in his
own being the new creation worked by Christ (2 Cor.
5:17) and then with open eyes to reflect on two immensely
sobering truths.

The first of these truths came home to him rather soon
after he began his apostolate. He came to see that the
reality that had claimed his life and called him to the
forefront of humanity had only a precarious hold on the
public life of man. When Paul looked upon his world and
then turned his gaze to the local churches, he saw the
appalling contrast between the task at hand and the
resources available. On the one hand, there were the great
promises of Christ in regard to the Church's task. "Go . . .

make disciples of all nations . . . and behold, I am with you all days, even unto the consummation" (Mt. 28:19–20). "Upon this rock I will build my Church, and the gates of hell shall not prevail" (Mt. 16:18). But for all these brave words, was there in Paul's lifetime, in a single Mediterranean city, one institution that had been changed for the better because Christians were in the city? Was public policy cleansed, or the morals of court life, or slavery, or the ritual corruption of the temples? And even if, in spite of lowliness, of poverty, of fewness, the early Christians insisted before authorities on their mandate to change all this, would they accomplish more than their own destruction? Was not the new faith therefore caught in a dilemma —either to play it safe in public, to build up a secret core of the elite and thereby risk becoming a mere faction or, on the other hand, to press its public claim and thereby risk extinction? It was a cruel dilemma, and Christian life has never entirely resolved it.

The second reflection of Paul would remind him that even the best disposed of his Christians were only beginners in the faith. In Paul's lifetime, the Church had hardly made a start in the task of forming Christians. There were flocks of Levantine freedmen, shopkeepers, the poor and uninstructed, the curious and lightminded. He speaks of them in his Letter to the Corinthians. "There were not many wise according to the flesh, not many mighty, not many noble" (1 Cor. 1:26). From the point of view of heroism or intelligence or depth of understanding, there were only a very few who could be counted on. There were men who had come to the faith for all sorts of reasons, men who were convinced that they were indeed Christians, when in fact the first contrary wind of discipline or reproof would reveal their fatuousness, their self-interest, their pharisaism.

The Church was hardly begun. Its dwelling within man

was so precarious, so unsure, that every moment brought
a danger of extinction. There were Christians on whom the
Church was unable to confer a conscience (Acts 5:1–11)
or honor (Acts 8:9–20). Many Christian lives were, in
fact, a contradiction in promise and deed, in the things
they prayed for and the things they would labor to bring
to pass. There were in the Church pagans who had baptized their paganism without abjuring it; they left in the
Galatian and Corinthian churches an unexpunged stain
of uncharity and false dealing and selfishness. Some Christians were determined to reform the community, even at
the cost of the annihilation of the community. Some were
determined on a widespread reform that would leave their
own inner lives unquestioned. Some would live at peace
only in a Church that reflected their image of what Christian life was. There were Christians who hastened into
action without prior thought and accomplished nothing.
And there were men of thought, with a native and stoic
disdain for action, in whom speculation dwelt like stale air
in a closed room, poisoning the atmosphere with its re-
fusals of life.

At the remove of many centuries, we recall the Pauline
definition of the Christian as a "new man" (Eph. 2:15);
Paul himself had reason to reflect soberly on the other side
of the coin. Every Christian in his world was a new Christian. There was not yet a single adult in the community
who had been born of Christian parents. All the believers
were rankly new. They were new about the altar; in
Corinth they brought their food to the Eucharist service,
overate and overdrank, and neglected the poor, who sat
unfed and disregarded in their midst (1 Cor. 11:33). The
Christians were new in the assumptions they brought to
the new faith. Many of them conceived of it as a baptized
pharisaism, a system in which the law saved man and

Christ was a mere appendage of Jewish history (Rom. 3:1). In Galatia, this situation was exacerbated by the preachers of a bastard faith, out of synagogue by the sanctuary, circumcised in body and unregenerate in mind, factionridden, contentious, a community of Judaizers and malcontents (Gal. 3:1–2).

Out of such material, how would one make a new race of men, endowed with love for their world, for God, for their neighbor? To human reasoning, the task would seem very nearly impossible. And yet it is precisely to this task that the "new men" had been summoned. It was the task to which Paul set himself and which by his lifetime's end had won its first success. We do well to reflect upon his tactic and method.

Liturgy and Action

The first tactic was deceptively simple, and in one sense it was still being forged in Paul's lifetime. It was liturgy. It was on the one hand a datum and a gift: "Go . . . baptizing them in the name of the Father, and of the Son, and of the Holy Spirit" (Mt. 28:19). "Whose sins you shall forgive, they are forgiven them" (Jn. 20:23). "This is my body, which is being given for you; do this in remembrance of me" (Lk. 22:19). But liturgy was, from another point of view, an action that demanded a human setting and conclusion. It included words and ceremonies to communicate correctly and understandably the full content of the august mysteries. It also implied activity in public life.

His letters were of great influence in helping the Church understand that both at the altar and in public a new stage of things had arrived. Before the conversion of Paul, the Church had had little practical experience of the full eucharistic mystery, the mystery that was destined to extend her consciousness of being universal. There was already a Palestinian liturgy, no doubt, but it had had as yet little effect in leading the Church into a practical exploration of her identity. Worship was still a localized affair, matched by a local apostolate. It was performed by Christians who were for the most part Jews. They were largely unaware, in any real sense, of a world mission (Acts 1:6, 15:5).

And this remains true, even though from the beginning both the oral traditions and the liturgical forms spoke of the Church as destined to become the body of humanity (Mk. 14:24, John 11:52). In spite of these great ideas, one cannot but note in practice a certain narrowness and parochialism in the Palestinian churches, a fear of the unknown, a practical unawareness that the Church must deliberately proceed to bring her redemptive gifts to all mankind (Acts 11:2–3).

The Church had experienced Christ, and she continued this experience in the Eucharist; but she had not yet experienced herself. She had not yet launched herself on the deep. She stood at that immeasurable and fearful moment when the whole future hangs in the balance, when an organism must decide whether it will take the risk of moving forward to the unknown, trusting in the forces of life that lie within it.

Church worship spoke of a universal act of reconciliation and love. The Eucharist brought to pass what the Lord had accomplished once for all on behalf of man in His death and victory. All this is true, but the question remained: was the Eucharist the whole task of the Church, and Palestine her only apostolate? The Lord had spoken in other terms: "Makes disciples of all nations" (Mt. 28:19). "You shall be witnesses for me in Jerusalem and in all Judea and Samaria and even to the very ends of the earth" (Acts 1:8).

The mandate was one thing, the acceptance of its full implications another. Even after Pentecost, the Church came with extreme difficulty to realize where her direction lay. Peter, who above all others might have been expected to understand, was in fact deeply unaware of the practical consequences of the words spoken by Christ at the moment of Ascension. He required a special vision to show him that the Church must announce salvation to the gentile world (Acts 1:10).

It was difficult to overcome the accumulated judgments that centuries of Jewish exclusiveness had formed in men. So stubborn were these prejudices that the Church might have found herself still in Palestine, debating her catholicity for several generations, had it not been for the Providential advent of Paul.

To realize the change he brought about is to realize how striking and operative is the effect on men of a symbolic action when that action is strongly joined to a life ideal. Paul's life is a reminder of something deeply true of human nature: no ideal can exert its full formative effect as long as men are unwilling to explore and experiment, working out its implications in life. And the principle remains true also of the religious life of man. Without a practical example before them, men are generally content to hear of an ideal as though it were merely a word, to ponder it as though it were merely a truth. They even grow content with a religion of inertia. They are willing to take part in their liturgy as though it were "pure" worship, uncontaminated by this world, deprived of historical implication, making no demands on them.

But it sometimes happens that the action of one man is of sufficient impact to close the gap that generally separates the words of men and their unexamined thinking. Such an action has the power of changing the thought of the whole community—sometimes by inviting revaluation,

sometimes by joining action to a neglected ideal, some
times by the simple process of awakening man's shame
through the contrast it sets up between selfless love and
community indifference.

The apostolate of Paul seems to have worked in some
what this way. His vocation to the gentiles, the break
through he worked to bring about, cast a new and fiercely
urgent light on aspects of the faith that men were in
danger of merely living with and practically neglecting
(Lk. 6:46). Paul showed that through the Eucharist the
Lord's death and victory had entered into every aspect of
man's life; his work, his marriage, his intellectual and cul
tural life—all were affected. The Eucharist could not, in
fact, be fully itself except as a ferment of redemptive ac
tion within man. Simply, the Eucharist was plenary when
its transforming energy brought man to give himself to the
works of Christ (Phil. 4:18). And to bring this to pass, a
simple, practical beginning was everything, as Paul saw.

One or two men must take ship, enter a foreign city,
mingle there with gentiles, show their human credentials,
debate, share, listen, make friends, announce the word,
show its organic unity with the hope of man, show in their
own persons the effect of the word of God on men; they
must show all this in a way that no man of goodwill
could ignore—with a passionate, insistent love of God and
men (Acts 8:4, 14:1, 16:11–15, 17:1–4). For the Eucharist
to be itself, the Church must become herself; for the
Church to become herself, so simple a thing must be done:
Christians must form a living procession from their altar
into their world. Hands must join, man must meet with
man—Jew with gentile, slave with freeman, rich with poor,
intellectual with workman. There was no other way.

By such a method, Paul joined the early Church's con
cern with her well-being to a concern with her task. And

the juncture is a crucial one, as experience shows. Too exclusive a concentration on personal existence, formulations of dogma, analyses of qualities and essence—these things may lead to a waste of life, a debilitation of energies unless air and light are let in on them from outside. To a sense of being the Church must join a sense of task, a work to be done, a sense of being unfinished in an unfinished world.

The relationship between an unfinished Church and an unfinished world is part of the adult awareness that Paul brought to the Church. Man is an imcomplete being in a world that awaits his hands. And the two realities, man and world, are not simply juxtaposed, as though either were static or totally outside the other, as though a joining of hands for mutual action would compromise the one or the other. The truth of the matter, as the Son of God had intimated in His incarnate presence, is a truth of mutual interpenetration. The unfinished world is the task of the Church; in loyalty to this task, the Church comes nearer her perfection. This is so deeply true that when the Church joins her concern for her own well-being to apostolic concern for the world, the fullest and holiest effects shortly come to pass, effects that are always predictable when her organism reaches out to join its own destiny with a larger hope.

Through the confident, daring action we speak of, the early Church discovered a sense of her own breadth, a sense that was immeasurably larger than her Palestinian forms. Through Paul's gentile apostolate, she came to see the obscure but luminous penumbra of her own future, a future that would progressively take on the form of the Lord's hope for her. "Go, therefore, and make disciples of all nations."

In sum, the world vision of Paul was the Providential instrument of God in protecting the Church from a double threat: the threat of pharisaism and of angelism. In this combat, Paul's view of the Church as a Body that is present and active in the world of man was a simple extension of eucharistic truth. The Body of Christ in its redemptive death and victory was made present to the Church in the community worship.

And the Eucharist built up the Church. There could be no least doubt that the two mysteries of Eucharist and Church were profoundly related (1 Cor. 10:17). Without the reality of the Eucharist to nourish and invigorate the mind of the Church, she would shortly fade to another of the disembodied, fastidious sects of history. She would lose her sense of relationship and responsibility to this world. She would lose her hopeful sense of her future, would become ossified in her Jewish beginnings.

It was the eucharistic mystery that broke this threat "This is my body, which is being given for you; do this in remembrance of me" (Lk. 22:19). Were ever believers introduced by way of mystery to a more real world? It was a world at whose center stood a real Body, veined with real Blood. "Bring here thy hand, and put it into my side" (Jn. 20:27). And this Body welcomed and sought relationships to real men, responsibilities toward them, since this Body had been "given for you," and the Blood "shed for you." And this sublime mystery of altruism contained the truth of the state of men; apart from this food and drink man was without hope, without love, without recourse in this world. "Unto the forgiveness of sins" (Mt. 26:28)— this was a statement that admitted man's dolorous existence and held to polluted lips his medicament.

Words were uttered across a table; bread and wine were distributed; healing, comfort, joy, strength were offered to man. From this burning center of existence, a center of all time and space, the Pauline mind faced its world. I shared with the gospel itself a common insistence. I

Christ, the life of God had descended to men; it had also been born in the midst of men. The Incarnate Word offered no comfort to unholy longings for a false peace. "And the Word was made flesh, and dwelt among us" (Jn. 1:14). "I write of . . . what we have heard, what we have seen . . . of the Word of Life" (1 Jn. 1:1).

To Paul, the equation was clear. If the Body upon the altar was a reality, so was the Body around the altar. Already the Body of Christ, the community was growing in dignity, growing in awareness of itself as a sacred, personal, and social being. And the Body of Christians was fitted by the eucharistic Body for this world. Indeed, there were two complementary processes taking place within the Church—one at the altar, one in the world. If it was true that the Bread of the altar was inducing growth in the Church, it must also be understood that mankind was inducing another sort of growth—a growth in understanding, in human gifts, in a sense of the world. And this was true to the extent that the Church could never be herself solely in Palestine any more than she could be herself solely about her altars.

The Church would become herself finally through submission to the destiny set for her by Christ—through the effort to bring this world to the saving truth of Christ. Christian fidelity could not be a matter solely of fidelity to the Eucharist. The truth of worship must expand into the truth of service, for Christ dwelt analogously both in the mystery of the altar and in the mystery of the neighbor. And in the effort of charity, the Church would come to a new understanding of the total mystery of Christ, which was the mystery of the cross, a service to man. "I die daily" (1 Cor. 15:31). "There is my daily pressing anxiety, the care of all the churches" (2 Cor. 11:28). "I bear the marks of the Lord Jesus in my body" (Gal. 6:17).

The death and victory of the Lord was renewed not

only on the altar but within men—in those who suffered
and in those who served. This death and victory would b
the continual gift of believers, given in Christ's name, t
all men. Christians would bear into their world a Eucha
rist assimilated to their bodily energies, to their sel
forgetfulness, to their sense of the Body of Christ—a Bod
which, as the Lord had made clear, was identified in i
destiny with the body of mankind (Mt. 28:19).

Somewhat in this way, through the Eucharist and th
Pauline example, the early Church answered the doubl
threat of pagan angelism and Judaic pharisaism. It was
solution that carried the community from its altar to i
world.

At the altar, the community was in process; it was be
coming what it witnessed and brought to pass. Throug
the Eucharist, it grew into the unity of Christ. "Becaus
the bread is one, we, though many, are one body, all of u
who partake of the one bread" (1 Cor. 10:17). And th
unity was no mere static protest against man's life. Implie
in this Church was an openness to ironies and opposition
an openness that marks every religious movement that rep
resents a new beginning within the destiny of humanit
So the Church, nourished by the Eucharist, was procee
ing into the world. The Eucharist, like a living fermen
in the bodies of men, made of the Church the ferment o
the body of mankind.

The relationship we speak of between the altar and th
world of man is insisted on early in Church history. Th
implication, as Paul declared, was that the believer wh
understood his worship would be impelled to act upo
his world. If he acted and spoke as a Christian durin
that action which is above all others the Christian ac
there would grow in him what Paul calls simply the "min
of Christ" (1 Cor. 2:16).

We can perhaps speak more exactly of the Christian mind as the Eucharist conferred it on believers. This cast of mind is a virile and measured optimism with regard to the world of man—a world that includes history, human enterprise, cultures, the form and coloration of the community of man. It is clear that Paul's thought moves in this direction. Christian discernment, clarified and deepened by grace, takes in the "learning of the Spirit" (1 Cor. 2:13); it "judges all things" (1 Cor. 2:15).

The term "Christian optimism" will repay reflection. Optimism is a Christian attitude chiefly through antimony. Human hope is Christianized when, from the point of view of grace, it is elevated to a theological virtue and when, from the point of view of human life, it finds itself under pressure—almost, one would say, under threat. This optimism is, in fact, the Christian response to the multiple pressures of circumstances beyond man's control, the unpredictable malice of man, pressures of the "power of darkness" (Col. 1:13). Optimism is the Christian reaction, finally, to the threat of God Himself (Lk. 12:49–53).

For God, as history witnesses, threatens Christian's belief in the goodness of their world by constantly allowing evil to try it. He forces men to hope against hope (Rom. 4:18). He allows their hope to be reduced to absurdity, that they might search out the breadth of merely human hope and then calmly surpass it. Providence forces Christians to question their own hopes, to see goodness submerged by the bitter tides of human circumstance (Lk. 24:38, Jn. 14:27). Under the lash and truncheon, under the failure of enterprise and the betrayal of trust, believers are commanded to stand firm in the conviction that, in these bitter circumstances, they are at length becoming Christian (Mt. 6:25).

Finally, Christian optimism is threatened by the de-

mands of Christian action. The point is made again and
again by Paul (1 Cor. 4:9, 2 Cor. 6:4ff., 1 Thess. 3:4, Phil
3:8). He is the enemy of the optimism that rests like an
unawakened infant in the nest of its own peace. There is
a kind of Christian optimism, he implies, that would be
destroyed by a single glance at the real world; certain
forms of hope have for their basis what any thinking man
would recognize as simple illusion (Gal. 3:1). The freeing of Christian life from illusion was a constant struggle
in the primitive Church; we are justified in saying that it
remains an even greater struggle in the Church today.

Christian Illusion and Crisis

Illusions of prolonged adolescence—the illusion that material affluence can define the heart of man; the illusion
that man can dedicate himself to the toys and distraction
of life without at the same time becoming his own judge
and executioner; the illusion that the neighbor is a free
option within human life, that one can "take man or leave
him" and still remain human—these are our burdens today.
The illusion is abroad that by some privilege unknown
either to Church or gospel, Christians are exempted from
involvement in the world.

It is this kind of optimism that is the death warrant of
reality. Among Christians it dwells in parochial minds
who measure all things by a traditional plumb line—the
line that joins a rectory to a school and to a series of comfortable interlocked streets. This is the nursery world of
the unawakened. Beyond is the terrifying unknown. And
within is pure dream.

And if we speak of what we might call the geometry of
mystery, the line that joins sacramental experience to human life, we would note a strange parallel to the geography of today's parish. The invisible line here would run

from baptistry to pulpit to altar and on to school and home. In many Christian lives, it would be a line drawn in early childhood and hewn to through all adulthood—a line that had deepened into a rut. In another sense, it is a line that has become a party line—it joins, man to man, the ethical, the cheerful, the interiorly pure, the good suburbanites. As clearly and jealously as a property line upon which taxes have been paid—and which therefore, by the logic of the suburbs, must be kept free from squatter man—this line traces for fathers and their children the limits beyond which the Christian vocation will not go, the limits it sets to its free action. A man could be baptized, shriven, take the Eucharist—and go through life seldom touching the real world. He would never serve the poor or the sick or the ignorant in any serious way; he would lead a sectarian pragmatic life and call it a religious life. He would never be troubled about the judgment of God on such a life; never experience anguish over "the world, the way it goes"; never sense the jealousy of God or the silence of God; never waver before the alternatives that mankind holds out—to choose, to renege, to refuse. Such a life has refused growth, refused to nourish others, refused to reproduce life. It is a life that, as Péguy has written, is skilled at turning even prayer and sacraments against God.

This line we speak of, rigid and inhuman, is drawn against the disturbing pressures of reality. Can a Catholic behind that drawn line hear a whisper through the barricades—a hint of strange tongues, a hint of men of color, a stench of poverty or disease, the commotion of a world other than the one he thinks is the real world? In such lives, is there a believer who cries out against his health as being more frightful than an illness? Is there one who has the courage to name a curse that which his century calls a cure—I mean the cure of the disease called man? Is there a Christian who can interpret the nightmare in which strange faces invade his heart—the black man whom daylight has kept at a distance but who comes at night with his claim in hand, his claim that man must sicken and die as long as he is immune from man? Is there one who knows that his nightmare is his only hope?

It is astounding when we reflect on the dissociation of seemingly "enlightened" Christians. Men who have read the Bible and taken the Body of Christ, men who know Shakespeare and Dante, men who have undergone the harsh experience of birth and illness and estrangement and death within their own family circle and come through it the better, men who, in sum, pride themselves on being conscious and adult and who are so esteemed by others—it is these men, the key men of the Christian future, who are sometimes hardest to understand.

They are undeniably good men. They pray, they reflect, they give of themselves. And yet when one has granted them everything they deserve, they still remain at a distance; they are less real than one had hoped. In the midst of their theoretic largeness, their charm, their good sense, an unknown quantity remains to trouble one.

The difficulty is not that they are men of ideas. Men of ideas are rare enough and badly needed at any time. But it is also clear that in every life a reductive process must begin somewhere, or the ideas that began by inducing life end by inducing death. When ideas remain too long unexercised, a man who begins as an intellectual, his mind in good trim, ends shapeless and useless in mind. His ideas grow sour or stale; they lead nowhere.

In the long run, such a man may know a great deal and understand a great deal. But one fault spoils everything And the fault is simply that a man may deny any claim on him from his own times. The fault is that he may glory in the history of man or the history of the Church as great ideas, but of his own times he may know nothing. The fault is that a man may not think his own times worth the price of knowing.

And let us not be deceived—the price of this knowledge is a heavy one. The price of knowing one's own times is always, to a Christian, the price of acting on behalf of one's times. Whereas the knowledge of the past, if it remains unconnected with man's present, has no price attached to it. It demands no living risks, neither the risk of misunderstanding nor of estrangement nor of practical mistake.

But to know the living is always a risky process. It implies the risks of a knowledge that must itself be living, since it centers on the living; that must be open, since the object of knowledge is the "other," and therefore changing, growing. This knowledge is, in the truest sense, of no mere objective "otherness" at all; it is a knowledge of someone whose immanence is always declaring itself, not before one's eyes or at arm's length but from within man's heart. So near is this other to one's own soul that to know him is to take the risk of knowing oneself; it is to take the risk, in rejecting the other, of rejecting oneself, of coming not to knowledge at all but to the denial of knowledge, to estrangement from one's own being.

And finally to know the living in the sense we speak of inevitably summons one to act on behalf of the living. To know the living is to hear the voice of the living. And this voice is, more often than not, importunate and, from the point of view of mere justice, undeserving. To know the living is to act on behalf of the living, because one hears in the voice of the living the first imperative of conscience— serve, be available for others.

Crisis and the Savior

The instinct we speak of, the passion to know and act, is not generally awakened by a system of thought or even by something so noble as a gift of prophecy or fidelity to a law. In the final analysis, it is only Christ who can say what is in man, who can release the sources of one's energies in man's favor. And He does this by the irresistible force of an act of love. "Jesus . . . having loved his own who were in the world, loved them to the end" (Jn. 13:1). "God so loved the world that he gave his only-begotten Son" (Jn. 3:16). "God is love" (1 Jn. 4:8).

It was in such an atmosphere, under the influence of such a life, that the outlines of the Christian sensibility first took shape. The Lord of eternity appeared in human life, and from the midst of men, from within the Body of a Man, He declared the goodness of all things. And this was no pronouncement lightly made in a tranquil hour. It was the triumphant reaction of heroic goodness to the entrenched forces of evil—an evil old as man himself, deeply seeded in history, having its source in an enmity properly satanic (Rom. 2:11, 3:23.)

In the face of this massive and feral power, the Son of God conquered by the simplest and most direct of expedients—by the gift of Himself (Jn. 13:1).

And the implication was clear to the believer. If history had evoked such love on the part of God, then history could not be entirely evil. If men had been so loved in spite of all the evidence of man's apostasy—an evidence of hatred, rebellion, and malice—mankind could not be entirely doomed to perish in its own evil.

We have suggested that this Christian hope, founded on the evidence of Christ's love and formed in believers by the Eucharist, is one of the chief tools in the Christian task. We could perhaps pause to ask in what way the Eucharist forms this viable hope in men.

It is clear first of all that the Eucharist is, in substance, both the crisis of the Savior's destiny and the resolution of that crisis. First the crisis: "And he, Son though he was, learned obedience from the things that he suffered" (Heb. 5:8). Then the resolution of crisis: "And when perfected, he became to all who obey him the cause of eternal salvation" (Heb. 5:9).

And this historical crisis of the Holy One is also the substance of man's crisis. In the Mass, that is, the Christian can discern a new shape taking form in human life. It is the new world of grace, the millennial curing of the ills that sin had effected.

Indeed, from Adam to Christ, sin had so completely passed into the history of mankind that man's existence could simply be summed up by saying, as Paul does, that man's state is a state of sin (Rom. 8:14–24). Human consciousness and human life were measurable by that darkness into whose depths man was born, in which he would die, without hope or love.

It is in reminding us of our desperation and guilt and in offering a way out that the Eucharist renews the crisis of the Savior in us. Will men accept the way to freedom? Will they accept the Father's will, as did His Son—accept that will, though it takes a shape neither attractive nor lucid nor humanly ennobling but simply the shape of holiness?

The first aspect of the crisis of the Savior was the Father's will. And this crisis, we suggest, is renewed in Christians through the Mass. But a further question is immediately implied: what is the Father's will with regard to man, and how can man discern it, given the unfinished and even chaotic nature of actual life?

The question immediately introduces us to the second element in the crisis of the Savior, an element implied in the Eucharist. If the first stage of the Savior's crisis brought Him to the Father's will, it must be added immediately that this will does not exercise itself in a vacuum. With respect to Christ, the Father's will was eminently historical. Its name was mankind (Jn. 6:39–40).

And this social aspect of the crisis of the Savior, as Paul was aware, is also the crisis of the Christian. "I rejoice now in the sufferings I bear for your sake; and what is lacking of the sufferings of Christ I fill up in my flesh for his body, which is the Church" (Col. 1:24).

In Paul's thought, mankind presents itself before Christians in the form of objective crisis—a future still in the breach, an imperceptible current of hope—which Christians can respond to or ignore. Charistian self-awareness includes three polarities that are objectively one: in the Christian, the identities of Christ, of the ego, and of mankind tend to merge. And the Pauline view of life insists that these three, taken together, form the "mind of Christ" in the adult believer. Man is fully Christian only when he is Christic man, and Christic man is man within mankind (1 Cor. 6:20). Christian consciousness, then, includes an awareness, at least in general terms, of the movement of man toward possession of himself and of his universe; of the destiny of man as man accepts it or mistakes it; of the scientific spirit and its formative pressures; of the struggle in which cultural forms germinate; of the welcome men must give to the hopes of other men—the welcome Catholics must give to Protestant hopes, to Negro hopes, to hopes that are simply human and therefore are ignored at the greatest peril; of the way Christians welcome all men into their hearts, seeing the hopes of mankind as the viable extension of their own hopes—sorrowing, loving on behalf of all; an awareness, also, of the way in which Christians destroy the hopes of men or put them off or explain them away or deny them a place within the consciousness of the Body of Christ. These are a few of the indices of that text which must be understood both as the text of the missal and as the text of man, a text which in both cases announces the continuing crisis of the Body of Christ.

The words of the Mass liturgy coincide with what we have called the text of man's hope. The liturgical word speaks of a universal hope, a universal redemption, a crisis already resolved in Christ and awaiting resolution in Christ's brethren. One thinks, in this regard, of a phrase of the prayer of offertory at Mass—"for all the faithful Christians, living and dead"—and, even more strikingly, of the words of the offering of the cup—"for our salvation, and that of the whole world."

According to a liturgical view of life, the world of man is in the breach; the Christian for whom liturgy is a living and lifegiving force enters this breach and, as far as can be done, works to close it.

One must admit, in the light of Church history, that the sense of crisis we speak of is often misunderstood by Christians. And this remains true even in the face of the summons that our faith issues to us—a summons to enter the crises of our society and to take part in their resolution. Our failure occurs in spite of the truth that our tradition and the life of grace itself teach us: that the love of God, communicated to us in Christ, endows Christians with an intense love and insight that could issue in decisions of enormous import to mankind.

Indeed, two influences are today picturing for us the true face of Christians as we appear to the men of our times. Within the Church, our prophets are men like Mounier, Murray, Roberts, Lynch, Mauriac, Suhard. From without, one must simply point to the march of world events and to the Christian gaps in the ranks of those who are working on behalf of intellectual and social change.

Both phenomena—the analyses given us by Christian prophets and the needs of mankind—speak of our frequent failure to grasp the realities of international life and of a mixed, complex society at home. They speak of our intellectual and artistic childishness, of our reactionary political tendencies, of the suspicion and resentment that arise among Catholics when the Church speaks in an adult way of world issues—as witness the reaction among many Catholics to the teachings of *Pacem in Terris* and *Mater et Magistra*. They speak of our prudent, sidelines approach to the struggles of the Negro, who is proceeding on his own schedule of integration, since so many Christians presumably have other interests than the Beatitudes. They speak, at least by implication, of our parishes, which are so seldom training centers for Christian action in the world. They speak of our distrust and fear of controversy, of our rigid, doctrinaire approach to truth.

Yet the Christian reality of grace has traditionally equipped men to see life clearly, to distinguish the real from its counterfeits, to read the events and movements of history as signs of Providence. Such men see themselves as protagonists within human life; they realize that the life of mankind and their own lives have met, that their lives are cast not only into the waters of baptism but into the tides of history as well.

What we might call the moment of recognition was a basic and powerful idea in ancient Greek drama. We recall that such a moment marked the true beginning of a life that deserved the dignity of the name human. Bringing man to this moment of truth were all the ironies and friendships and enmities and pressures of a life that had previously presumed to be human but was in fact lost in darkness. Such a life was often symbolized under the image of physical blindness. The hero moved toward a fate of

which he knew nothing. He had to substitute all sorts of
devices for the living eye of sight; he felt his way with a
stick, he leaned upon children or the old. Because he had
lost his sight, and often his way as well, he depended on
those whose adult life was presumably nearing its end or
had not yet begun. The voices of prophecy, of history, of
conscience, and of the neighbor reached him in a void.
They were like the voices that shout into the ear of the
dead. Until the moment of recognition, all the signposts
and soundings by which man learns who he is and where
he is bound are denied him.

And this remains true of the Christian as well as of the
pagan. Until he has seen life in a human way, he remains undifferentiated, amoral, and factitious. He recedes
to the world of objects and blind forces and process; he is
one with a world whose very being is blindness. If the
voices of other men reach him, they are by definition the
voices of strangers; by presumption they are even hostile.
The voice of conscience and the voice of events are alike
dead texts, untranslatable. Does the voice of God reach
such a man? It hardly can, for to him God's voice is one
which above all others must not be trusted or hearkened
to. For this voice presumes to be the first and only voice
—to speak from within the universe, from within nature,
from within the neighbor, from within man's own heart
(Rom. 1:20). And it commands: "I am the Almighty God:
walk before me, and be perfect" (Gen. 17:1).

How shall such blindness be healed? God's word assures
us that it can be healed, but only from on high, by a
moment of recognition. It can be healed only in Christ. "I
am the light of the world. He who follows me does not
walk in the darkness" (Jn. 8:12).

It is this moment of recognition that the liturgy of the
Church gently and hopefully works to bring about. Her

first prayer over the new Christian indicates this: "May Thy son serve Thee gladly in Thy Church." The prayer is more than a pious wish; it is the effect that the Sacrament brings to pass—unity, restoration, love.

Pagan man had been given over to an impersonal world governed by the hatred of Satan, a world of disenchantment and divorce, a universe of haphazard brutality (2 Cor. 6:16). But now man is summoned "to serve the living God." He is invited to a gentle, organic healing, to a filiation, to a friendship. As the love of God for man is declared and effected anew, the believer is led by the hand, a newly cured blind man, into the midst of a circle of light and warmth, a human family, to serve God in His Church. It is a moment of recognition—man comes forward to know his universe and to be known there, to recognize the real world and to be recognized there.

There is a passage in St. John which, we are told, was possibly composed as a baptismal reading. The Lord who is the Light of the world stooped to take some clay into His hands, moistened it with spittle, rubbed it upon the eyes of a man born blind, and commanded him to go and bathe in the waters of the pool of Siloe. And the man went, John tells us, and bathed, and he returned seeing (Jn. 9). It is a gentle parable of the healing that issues from the waters of the Sacrament to touch the blind—the blind in sight and heart, those who, in the Greek sense, have missed the way of life.

The tenderest moment of the episode was reached when the man returned to kneel at the feet of the Savior; the words of recognition bring us the inmost meaning of the passage: "Jesus . . . said to him, 'Dost thou believe in the Son of God?' He answered and said, 'Who is he, Lord, that I may believe in him?' And Jesus said to him, 'Thou hast both seen him, and he it is who speaks with thee.'

And he said, 'I believe, Lord.' And falling down, he worshiped him" (Jn. 9:35–38).

The true restoration, in the intention of the Lord, was the moment of faith. It was that moment which summoned the blind man—and all men—into God's presence for the healing of his compounded blindness. And in that healing, the man born blind recognized at one stroke his God, his brethren, and himself. He had been cured of a blindness that had both for subject and content man himself—man bereft of God, of his brother, and of his own soul.

The glance of the man who was healed rested in the face of the Friend of man (Jn. 9:36). And in the lineaments of that face, he saw his own. He saw his own face—and how much more. In the face of Christ, he saw a universe, a universe charged with inner life and love. A universe which, like a single human face, would be thinned by time to the very bone; it would be thinned like a shell to resonate, with ever more refined and piercing notes, the harmony of the spheres.

And the man who was healed of blindness saw in Christ's face not merely the shape of all things that are but the shape of all that ever was or would be. He saw all time consecrated to the immortality of the face of man, to the shape it would wear in the vision of God. Unborn, malleable in the womb of a woman, or a broken skull, a fragment of time's detritus—it made no difference. In the moment of recognition, man knew man—his temporality and his diuturnity, unborn and long dead, relic and portent, neighbor and self, man and mankind.

Could all men see what man must see; that the sight of one face would heal the blindness of the universe. This is what St. Paul declares: the radiant majesty of the Father shines in the face of Christ (2 Cor. 4:6). In His face have met all the human feelings of patience and hope and altruism and sacrificial love that were scattered like leaves before a storm at the time of the Fall. Now the text is gathered and bound in one; it is written on a human heart and shines from a human face. "I am the Alpha and the Omega, the first and the last, the beginning and the end" (Apoc. 22:13).

Christians are those, it has been said, who can read this text aright. This is their special glory; it belongs only to them. Only they are equipped, by the gift of God, to take up and read and recognize. And the reading of the text, it goes without saying, is not merely a historical or artistic exercise, not a gesture before the Christ of history or a submission to academic truth.

Neither is this moment of recognition something to be delayed until the last day. Rather, it is a present encounter, an exercise of each hour. To every man, the summons has come; in his credo to Christ, man is called to say his credo to humanity. "Saul, Saul, why doest thou persecute me?" (Acts 9:4). "I am the vine, you are the branches" (Jn. 15:5). "I was hungry and you gave me to eat . . . thirsty and you gave me to drink" (Mt. 25:35). "As long as you did it for one of these, the least of my brethren, you did it for me" (Mt. 25:40). "We are members of his body, made from his flesh and from his bones" (Eph. 5:30). The Christian power of recognition rests on the world of man, acknowledges a viable nexus with Him who continues within mankind the mystery of His own completion.

8. Man's Spirit and Technology

As we undertake our topic, the facts of modern life serve to modify our observations, qualified as our thought must be by the mutual relationships arising between technology and religion. In the first place, the contact of technologists with the world of theology is a very distant one indeed. Technologists are not normally aware that theology is of any relevance or has a tradition of its own. And, conversely, up to the present, theologians have stood only on the outer fringes of the new world which is developing around them. Intramural interests and the suspicions engendered by history have thus kept each side at a distance from the other. The estrangement, it must be added, continues, at the expense of unity of experience and sympathetic universalism; it continues even though in times past men recognized no outer world beyond the sacred and no inner world consecrated in principle to the secular.

Indeed times have changed. The old unity of men has broken up. Theology, as someone has said, has been robbed of its capital letter, and science has had one conferred on it. The ideal of a transcendent unity in which human knowledge was suspended, illumined, and directed has all but vanished. Philosophies of life and theories of knowledge have proliferated until their common sources are uncovered only with extreme difficulty. Again, no theologian with his eye to his world will claim to speak for any but a very small number; beyond his own community, his words are weighed, debated, or ignored with quite the same sangfroid as greets any enthusiast or theorist whose credentials have not passed muster.

And not only are religious claims rarely taken with seriousness by men of the world. A very profound trouble afflicts the religious families themselves. Theologians are free to speak for their own house, but they do so conscious that no one of their dwellings is at peace with itself. The winds of world unrest and change have ripped through the churches, shaking their very foundations. Among thinking men of faith, and especially among the young, there is a profound unrest. Indeed, the questioning in the air leaves nothing untouched; motives, social conscience, forms of community, the nature of faith, the existence of God, the relations of institutions to freedom—all are up for debate. An agonizing effort is under way to analyze the religious soul—an effort, one might almost say, to form a new religious soul, by men who are conscious of their inner poverty, their sinfulness, the painfully obscure faith that is their only resource.

All this is certainly vexing, but I would venture to call it also extremely hopeful. It can at least be said that the troubling of the waters saves us who must walk them from a profound folly which in times past kept us both arrogant and ignorant. We were arrogant before upheavals that we presumed would shake all but our mighty fortress; we were ignorant of the language of our Bible, which speaks of the life of faith as a painful and exigent form of servanthood in the world. Such ignorance is happily reduced by the facts of present life—the present upheavals have brought the realization that we have fewer answers than we thought. So we are at least less apt to be victimized by illusion as we take our place with struggling men, trying with them to understand a world change that seems to leave nothing inviolate.

The change we are witness to, it must be insisted, is changing men even as men transform the world. Man is coming to know better that he must bear the responsibility for his new knowledge and for its consequences. He cannot by an act of the will or an act of virtue unlearn nuclear secrets or recoil from outer space. No true unity, either in human consciousness or in mankind at large, can be gained by an effort to return to the womb of innocence or of the past. The new discoveries are irrevocably ours; they are part of the patrimony of man, as is Greek rationalism or the Parthenon or plainchant or the insights of Freud or the art of Picasso. Such achievements are simply to be welcomed, to be integrated with conscience and mind, to be evaluated in the light of everything that produced them and of everything they may be expected to produce.

The task of an integration of experience is always terrifyingly obscure. How indeed does mankind assimilate new forms of knowledge in a way that sustains new relationships with others? By what moral and intellectual consensus is new knowledge controlled in its aims, in a way that will reduce tensions instead of exacerbating them? What moral factors, what new insights into the future will summon the genie from the bottle—to serve rather than to destroy?

Evidently the kind of integration we speak of is possible to Western society. Indeed, it is part of our glory. Western history has insisted that violent shifts in man's relation to time are part of historical process itself; in art or political change or technical discoveries, there is no simple escalation upward into the good life. In the West, paradoxically, the changes that count have occurred through revolution. And revolution, whether it occurred within the nation-state or in world society, has been presumed to lie under the control of the men who brought it to pass. Sometimes during the upheavals, sometimes after their violence had been spent, such movements of change were brought under the judgment of the community. Change was always seen as part of history itself—sometimes violent and chaotic, sometimes gradual, but always as controllable by judgment and conscience. Revolutions may have brought new freedom in their wake, they may have suppressed freedom; they may have opened new horizons to spirit, or they may have cut them back. But invariably they were subject to a critique of reason or to an admission of guilt.

In such a way, historic change offered the occasion for a renewal of consciousness itself. Men who underwent change were responsible for the integration of change into life. Revolutions stood under the most tenacious of human presuppositions—the suppositions that social change must be ordered to the common good; that in an atmosphere charged with revolution, man cannot act without responsibility or submit without judgment. Such a willingness to judge and be judged, to seek out a consensus, and to listen to others implied, from a negative point of view, that a world of irresponsibility is also an inhuman world. It implied, pushing the matter to an extreme, that the greatest absurdity conceivable is a world in which turmoil and chaos have become values in themselves, autonomous, unpredictable, uncontrolled.

The absurdity and horror implicit in the loss of control over events must not, moreover, be thought of as merely a conclusion that history has forced on man. Something far deeper is in question here. The truth that man belongs responsibly in the world expresses, in fact, a passionate sense of being, a sense of order. Man knows, even obscurely, that he is called to create the world, which is both outside him and within him. He cannot evade his dominion over creation without destroying himself. In the biological order of things, he comes up through this world, body and spirit. He is born of its times and its seasons, he breathes its atmosphere, and events force him to make judgments. And the biological facts of life are a symbol of spiritual truth. Through others, through action, through responsibility, man comes to imagine the real. Through these things, he may even come to entrust himself to it.

Man and the world form a moral unity. And man is forbidden to destroy this harmony. The law is a conclusion of his active power of touching reality in history, of forming his future, and of rejecting the chimeras and the moral folly that would threaten his existence. Man conceives of a beginning of the world that coincides with his own beginnings. He can conceive of an end of things that includes his own last day. But he cannot imagine, without doing violence to his being, a world of order or meaning perduring without him. He finds senseless and horrifying the notion of a posthuman universe. That is, no event from within the world, issuing from human minds and executed with human hands, can be accepted as ending human existence.

Our conclusion is not merely an imaginative recoiling; it is also a moral one. Man's almost infinite capacity for living with crime and pain and sin and wars has allowed him to pick up the pieces after almost any catastrophe and to go on—as the Second World War and Dresden and Hiroshima and Sharpeville witness. But he cannot consent to his extinction, self-willed, executed by his own powers, as a hypothesis that could be called a moral hypothesis.

It is perhaps necessary to begin our reflections with these remarks in order to set off our present situation from any crisis that has gone before. No revolution, no scientific breakthrough prior to our own generation—nor all of them taken in their sum—could have brought us to the brink where we stand today. There was never before a time,

that is, when men could announce the simple power to
end time, to end man, to end history, to bring down the
world. Every prior crisis granted, at very least, space for
the unborn, an inhabitable area for the majority, blueprints for the future—in short, some trace of cultural vision,
living men, and purpose issuing from ruin.

With the threat we now lie under, no such luxury is
granted us. Technology, as no one needs to be told, has
introduced on the scene an altogether new possibility in
the form of total war. The news at its deepest is not military news or even philosophic news. It is a question of the
will of God and the will of man meeting at a new point of
human advance. Who of us was not struck cold at the heart
when the first atomic bomb was unleashed on Japan?
Our moral existence, our relationships to other men, our
guilt took on an entirely new form. We knew, and we
could never forget, that we had experimented with mankind in the test tube of a great city.

One cannot insist too strongly on the ominous form
which events since then have taken, especially the cold-
war developments in which technology has had such large
part. The nuclear buildup has in fact hardened the drive
of technological man to seize to himself certain moments
that believers have always recognized as God's.

Undoubtedly, investigation will continue to cast more
light on the account of creation contained in the Book of
Genesis. But a certain sense of mystery will always remain; the account of the creation of man occupies a very
special place in this tradition. Human life, that is, is God's
gift and prerogative; it is a sharing in divine activity, a mode
of God's presence in the world. Man is the apple of His eye.
He is invited to dominate and people the earth, is summoned
to self-realization and unity and love. And an end of things is
obscurely hinted at—an end that will be clarified through-

out history and the growth of sacred tradition. It indicates that a mysterious last day will occur, the full flowering of the process which creation has entrusted to man but which God must enter to fulfill. In such a way, both God and man govern the end of things—man by bringing creation to a certain fullness, God by intervening to judge history and its works, to welcome men into beatitude.

And throughout history, as the Bible bears witness, sin is always present. Human advance is brought about by sinful men, by men who are forced to live with the deepest perplexities and the most painful choices as they assume responsibility for their world. Man must live with his questions, he must live even with his sinfulness, conscious that sinless activity is an ideal rather than a fact, knowing that sin is part of the mystery of human wills operating concretely in time, knowing finally that even sin serves.

Meantime, throughout all time, the questions remain. Is man, on a given occasion, acting in accord with moral order? Is man moving forward, under the light of reason, toward the fuller good of his being and the good of community? Or is he indulging his ego in a Promethean and destructive way, leveling all before him in obedience to the dark forces of pride?

History offers some light, after the fact at least, on these questions. It offers certain broad areas for judgment upon political, scientific, and social change. We have no difficulty as moral beings in judging Hilter's racism or apartheid or the event at Hiroshima or Stalin's genocide policies. What Gabriel Marcel calls a "deep sense of piety toward life" comes to our aid in qualifying such horrors. Marcel goes on to say, "It is in connection with this spontaneous piety, as an outrage against it, and more often than not, quite independently of any positive religious attachment, of any link with historical revelation, that these acts, which we have been the witness or victims of, seem to us to bear the undeniable marks of sin."

But a different irony, or at least a modifying irony, stands clear in today's effort to bend technology to war. It has something to do with a nearly total loss of confidence in the forces of spirit, and a nearly total confidence placed in the forces of technique. The two attitudes, let us not hesitate to say, are complementary as excesses and deficiencies. Jacques Maritain has remarked on this perversion of the forces of spirit and matter and of their harmonious interaction in the world. Today, the harmony is broken. It is no longer possible to speak of spirit as self-directive, of moving ahead of matter and subjecting it to moral control. Neither is it possible to imagine that material forces, given our world and its atmosphere, will submit to such control. Technologists are more and more impatient of such talk, if indeed they hear it at all. For man has broken through, and the breakthrough is not merely scientific. It marks momentous change within man, in his relationships to his fellows, to his world, to God. One is reminded of the way in which Greek tragedy saw man as brought to crisis by the sin of *hubris*—the overstepping of human limits, the perverse effort to play god. And one thinks also of the Hebrew account of the Fall—the temptation to cast off the burden of creaturehood, to assume moral control of the universe. Some obscure parallel, one thinks, joins these ancient myths to our own days.

Tentativeness, a sense of purpose joined to the good of all, an attitude that steps softly in unknown areas—these are no longer considered crucial to man's effort to transform the world. Scientific effort spirals upward, narrowing toward a cone; at the vent stands one man's control or one nation's pride. In such a process, the good of the person and the good of the community are inevitably obscured as values and goals. In the atmosphere of the cold war, more-over, each stage of the process is looked on as a value in itself, a kind of teasing invitation. We have gotten so far, why not further? Since a breakthrough has happened, why not a further one? Beyond any reasonable doubt, a further one is desirable. Let us make it.

Given the world atmosphere of the last twenty years, the ruin lurking in such a rationale grows more and more visible to thinking men. The ruin is implied in the nature of things. No revolution, including the technological one, can occur in a historical vacuum; ours has been taking place during a period when the passions of nationalism, pride, and isolation are at fever heat. At the same time, local wars have erupted throughout many parts of the world, allowing both sides logically to harden positions, covertly or openly to take sides, to probe the weak spots in the other's armory, to keep terrors, recriminations, and threats boiling—even, on one or two occasions, to bring the superpowers almost to the point of no return.

Our topic cannot therefore be realistically considered apart from the fact of the cold war. In the past twenty years, technique and science have been applied in the first place to war and war preparation. It must be said quite simply that such activity has not merely deflected world resources and arrested world development; something far more serious is at stake. Cold-war technology is, in fact, a deliberate and enormously effective assault on man's spirit. Its contempt for man is expressed in its working assumption; when the forces of nature are brought to a certain point of useful control, literally nothing is forbidden—no further step, no bigger bomb, no passage from nuclear to hydrogen weaponry, no inclusion of larger populations and larger land units in the calculations of death. In such ways, war technique implements its contempt for reason; it mounts a world arsenal built on the poverty of the multitudes, debases the moral sense of men with a massive propaganda of self-justification, narrows the freedom and breadth of human inquiry to a dark single-minded obsession. Its contempt for man assigns him finally only two possibilities; destruction or the arms race. These are the Neanderthal alternatives offered to a mankind of infinite resources. Their symbols are those of hideout and counterforce—the London tube shelters of the Second World War and the saturation bombing of the German cities, the shotgun at the shelter door and the nuclear atmospheric-testing programs.

It is this appalling limitation of human possibility, brought about by techniques that had promised men all heaven and earth, that must give pause to thinking men. As we suggested, cold-war technology condemns man to the underground or to programs of destruction above-ground. Ironically, this same technology had promised man a new freedom from his ancient bondage to time and this world. But it has in fact brought no such freedom; it has enslaved the spirit of man to a degree that cruder societies had never attempted. The enslavement is in the air; it is a poison of dread and restraint, a counterpoint of unlimited violence, a dread of existence, a waste of psychic energy. It implies the destruction of that sense of tradition in which man was free to draw on his past in order to form a human future. But now, under the nuclear shadow, who is certain of any future at all?

Yet the spirit has its own reality, which can never be entirely destroyed. Spirit speaks of possibility, of a sacred overflow of truth and beauty, of resources of altruism, of the passionate tendency of man to give himself and in his gift to renew himself, of love without measure or limit, of moral dominion over a servant universe, of an infinite hunger to be and to become, to imagine and to trust the world.

Technology too has its definition, not to be confused with its uses. It is in fact the servant universe itself, the forces of nature existing on behalf of man. It includes procedures of knowledge, methods of determining the forces at the disposal of intelligence, of organizing and exploiting these forces. These are the general procedures that our own age has brought to a brilliant climax.

Such technique has promised us very great things; sometimes we have even had a glimpse of what the new resources of knowledge, rightly used, can do for us in medical, engineering, biological, and cultural areas. We can only mourn the fact that the uses of peace have been secondary to the uses of war, that man's brilliant technological advance has been so tardily and penuriously put to the kind of service that could be called human.

Indeed, had not technology been seized on by the cold war, by war making and war preparation, what a different tone our reflections on technique and spirit would take! We undoubtedly would have cause to rejoice at medical, biological, and engineering discoveries of the highest importance, the discoveries of man used in the service of man. Our reflections would express the serenity of religious humanists; they would reflect a conviction that we could see taking actual shape around us, a conviction that the future belongs actually to those who have created it, that time is escalating human achievement into greater triumphs, that times of peace are allowing all men—technicians and world leaders, believers and unbelievers—to share and plan for the universal good.

We need mention the possibilities only in order to pass beyond them. The golden age of man, no matter how fervently we might have hoped that it would take a technological form, simply has not occurred. Only here and there, as a kind of extracurricular effort, compassion and technique have broken through—in the efforts of specialist teams abroad, in the foreign-aid programs of the Western and Eastern governments. But in comparison with war efforts, these have been little more than distractions or interludes. They have never seriously interfered with the arms race or allowed men to forget that the main issue of the world today is not man as a friend and brother but man the enemy.

For all of us, this period of war preparation and the expending of ingenuity and resources into war is hard and exhausting indeed. None of us has been left untouched by the angel of death. For the poor, its touch is further poverty; for the affluent, it is neurosis, estrangement, acedia, despair. Technology in military uniform has claimed our laboratories and research centers and universities. Its shadow has lain heavily on the nights and days of our political leaders.

In such an atmosphere, something even more destructive and mysterious has occurred. A radical permeating change in the atmosphere of life has slowly brought about a profound change in man himself. A climate of war creates its own horizons, its own justification and method. Subjected to such an atmosphere for a long period of time, men come to accept it as normal and self-evident; they create a logic that suits their state of soul. They create tools of violence as entirely normal methods of dealing with "the enemy"; once created, the tools are used with ever-increasing ease. Peaceableness, communication with others, discussion, public candor—these are less and less trusted as methods of dealing with human differences. The cold war dictates its own methods and progressively outlaws the possibility of other methods.

In such an atmosphere, men gradually come to accept a totally different version of human life. Their capacity for perceiving goodness and truth and of acting on their insights is impaired. Their convictions about who they are become transformed into illusions expressing only what they once were or what they wish they could be. They react with unhealthy sensitivity to the criticism of others— even their friends and allies. Such men live in the dream-world of the schizoid or the adolescent, their sense of identity victimized by its controlled sources. The stranger becomes the enemy; the enemy is everywhere. His image tends more and more to harden into an absolute, beyond redemption, beyond change, implacable, unappeasable. And almost inevitably, as the complexities of human relationships merge into the single image of the enemy, a complementary image of ourselves arises. We become the beleaguered defenders of all that is good and noble in life, the society that can do no wrong, whose interventions are always governed by superior wisdom, whose military might serves only the good of humanity. Goodness and evil—two profoundly abstract, obsessive, unreal images —thus tend to replace the necessary, ongoing, and untidy process of human relations.

The war atmosphere also tends to restrict the activity of those who could, in normal circumstances, bring relief to our illness. The restrictions against peacemaking operate in many ways. They narrow the imaginative possibilities, suggesting constantly that solutions to our difficulties lie beyond the capacities of nonspecialists. Gradually, men whose capacities lie outside the iron categories of the moment grow discouraged. They no longer see themselves in a healing role, invited to think through the responsibilities that their gifts fit them for. Thus the cold-war climate tends to restrict the works of peace and direct them into a channel that is strictly controllable. Peacemaking, which is the profound and first issue of modern times and the first capacity of healthy men, is no longer seen as spiritual power, capable of bringing violence under the control of reason. The work of peace no longer belongs in any true sense to the people—to the artists, the philosophers, the historians, to those men whose disciplines have given them important, even irreplaceable insights into the meaning of man and his society. Gradually, the task of peace is withdrawn from the churches also; in time, they no longer think even to claim it. The keeping of the peace thus inevitably becomes the speciality of small groups of diplomats and military experts, operating in secrecy, less and less answerable to public opinion. They control the peace by controlling the means of war. So we come full circle to the absurdity with which, one may presume, the first arrow was launched at the first enemy. In order to make peace, one prepares for and wages war.

An absurd and terrifying world thus becomes our real world. None other exists. Believing men inhabit it side by side with the unbelieving. Believing men work within it, sometimes ineptly, sometimes heroically, sometimes in a growing despair. In that world, much that we could say to other men, much that we could hope for from them and ourselves, goes unsaid or goes underground or, by a kind of mutual gentleman's agreement, is suppressed. A sense of compassion for a sick world is forbidden its operation. And by the same rule, our own sickness goes largely undiagnosed and unhealed. Men on both sides lie wounded and despoiled, but very few are permitted to pause and assuage and console. Travel and free exchange with large parts of the world are proscribed. The intellectual and cultural and scientific communities either join the war effort or are no longer consulted. And when protest arises, those in power react as though disloyalty or even treason were in the air. In such a way, the critique of society, which can go forward only in communion with all its members, is halted. Americans tend more and more to accept a view of themselves which has been sternly defined for them, somewhat like an order of the day in a city under siege. The clichés and fears of nationalism, operating in ignorance of the world, are the primary teachers. Such slogans tell us, indeed, that we have every right to be respected and loved, to be regarded as generous and peaceable and large-minded. But the world, when it can be heard, has other news for us.

Can believers help break this impasse? We know that throughout history, certain of them have broken through the narrow confines of state loyalty with the liberation that God's word offers men. We believe that the same service can be offered today; indeed, in the life of Pope John, we have a radiant example of just this form of Christian activity. Today, the need of a consensus of enlightened men, a consensus that will include the voice of Christians, is desperately needed. But we know, too, that what we have to say to the world cannot be said from a distance. We cannot retreat to theological barricades in order to announce that technology in the service of war is the active enemy of man's spirit. Such a retreat places in question the sincerity of those who speak. The world can be healed, as the Bible makes clear, only by those who take its own flesh.

Yet, our standing in the world, our sense of sharing its anguish, our looking together with all men into the abyss, is not an agreement to see only what the world sees or to agree with the world's conclusions about ways of bridging the void. The state of conformity, says Simone Weil, is no more than an imitation of the state of grace. The decision to live with others and to welcome their vision of life to our own does not imply that our vision coincides at every point with theirs. Believers who take their stand in the world at the same time reserve the right to quarrel with, modify, or even disclaim the world's reasons for its own fidelity. Only such a stance, that of love of our times and fidelity to faith, can lend us the qualifications for responsible action.

The world's need of Christians could perhaps be defined as a need for spiritual presence and a need for prophecy. The prophecy required of us is one that has undergone the experience of the world and hence can speak out of knowledge and compassion rather than from safety or distance. And the Christian presence must also be carefully understood; it is a presence filled with spirit rather than merely another technique among techniques; it is a sense of man, in fact, which admits of a breakthrough from without.

We believe the Christians can offer the world precisely this mode of presence and this insight into events. But our claim is logical and useful only if it takes into account our responsibility to know the world—to undergo its terrifying crises, to stand at the side of perplexed and hard-pressed men. Only such a religion, seeking to live in the world, can claim to be a religion of the world, a religion for men. Applied to our present concern, such Christianity is not exempted from knowledge of the complexities of the cold war; it is only through such knowledge that the "searching of the Scripture" will yield us new light on His will. In fidelity to both sources of wisdom, to life in the world and to life in God, an approach will be found. I will not say an approach to a solution, which implies that faith may be merely a superior form of problem solving, but an approach to light and liberation.

That technology itself cannot grant this light to man's future or open this door needs no proof. Technique has already been offered a rather long period of time to present its version of human life. And across the world in the last twenty years, technology has served neither freedom nor peace; it has served the cold war. It has afforded another example (the more shocking since the means at hand are now literally without limit) of the fascination that technical progress holds for men. It is a fascination that has become an obsession; in all seriousness, men pursue a single, highly questionable goal at the expense of man himself.

These reflections are in no sense offered in order to draw moral lines that exclude ourselves from guilt. Believers stand within the cold war; we are part of it. In each of our crises and their gradually narrowing alternatives, we are in measure implicated. Technologists knew of no principle of control of technique, and their work brought them very little light on the existence of such a principle. The failure of effective control, the failure of a vision of man, lies at least in measure at the door of those who have at their disposal a tradition of conscience and who, for whatever reasons, failed to communicate—who failed, in most instances, even to protest.

In this failure, which is a common failure, it can at least be seen that a fuller understanding of the limits of technology is becoming clear. Technique has been organized in view of a task it could never in fact accomplish. Given the fact of sinful men in the world, given the cold-war ideologies of nationalism and pride, technology could not guarantee the peace of the world. The failure is a parable that may even admit of a wider application. Technology will never in any case guarantee the good life, whatever form man's future may take. The one failure, that of the last twenty years, must in all seriousness be taken as the corollary of the other. We cannot suppose that is, that if only we get over the hump of the cold war and apply the techniques we have learned to the needs of world society, all will be well.

The failure of the peace in a world that had seemed to promise everything is, we suggest, the symbol of a failure whose outlines are all but lost in the brutal war landscape of the present world. It is a failure of vision; it will continue to haunt us in peace also. Indeed, if the cold war is halted, what of technological society in peace? The question takes on growing urgency as it becomes clearer that some form of universal peace is the only practical alternative to world destruction and as the men who have staked everything on serving the iron necessities of the cold war come to realize that their usefulness must inevitably take another form.

Technology as war, we have insisted, is regressive and monstrously destructive. But what of technology as peace? Is war an embolism in a healthy body that can eventually heal its own disease and restore itself? Or is the body of man, which is now a technological body, no more than an organized pandemic illness? Before we attempt an answer, our reflections must carry us courageously into the facts of modern life, facts that are directly connected with a technical civilization. We must think of the ennui and waste that afflict the rich societies, of their inequities, their failure to care for their own victims, their inability to use their comfort and affluence as a source of new responsibility. We think of the attrition that urban life exerts on the energies and hopes of the majority; of the racial hatreds that simmer and boil to the surface of those societies; of the impoverishment of imagination as men stand powerless before the rigors of personal and social life, unable or unwilling to apply the techniques of healing to the despair of their neighbors. We think of the debasement of taste and the loss of moral energies of rich and poor alike through canned entertainment, the triviality of mass attitudes, the massive moral inertia symbolized by retreat from life, by cynicism, by idolatry of structures, by fear, by the loss of what Dewey calls "piety toward experience."

Armaments indeed are not our only difficulty. To single them out as the present greatest danger to man is only to reflect on their symbolic content, to realize that they stand as symbols of all the objects men place around themselves to mirror the state of their soul. That state of soul appalls us as it fashions for its chief art objects the merciless engines of death standing in our underground galleries.

But what form will the artifacts of the age of peace take? We are not left entirely in the dark, thanks to the social engineers and the planners. Machines for artificial insemination, machines for the manipulation of the nervous system, machines for the elimination of undersirables, machines of universal control of life from the test tube to the grave—such are the blueprints of the social architects, joining a primitive, destructive naïveté to our worst nightmares.

The elimination of war and of preparation for war would be an act of the highest order, in favor of mankind. But even were war solemnly abjured as an effective instrument of justice, the real question, from which warmaking has been the great historic distraction, still remains. It encompasses the uses of the new technology in peace as well as in war. What is man, anyway?

9. New World, New Forms of Faith

TODAY, AS THROUGHOUT history, the world is something very real to believers. Their Bible, one might say, comes out of it. In the world, God has made Himself known, first through the prophets and then, as Christians believe, through the presence of His Son. The world is thus a very special focus of God's action, from the beginning to the end of time. It stands for that excellent creation upon which the eyes of Love rested, which He found good, which He blessed with a mounting wave of life that culminated in consciousness, in man. And because God has found it good, the world continues to witness to the glory of God in a way that cannot finally be defaced or obscured. Creation is an ordered work of the divine wisdom and beauty. God's power shines through it; it is charged with His grandeur, the poet says. So man is awakened to acts of admiration and praise; he responds to God in and through the contemplation of His world.

And he turns to his fellow men and discovers himself anew in them. Indeed, apart from others, his knowledge risks delusions and emptiness, and his capacity for love hangs in the void. Man is created to know and love not only God but men. Man's social needs are powerfully represented in the Book of Genesis, where he finds himself at the beginning, alone, radically incomplete. Then, a mysterious other person is drawn from his being, breathed upon, and set at his side. She is to be the companion of his hope, the source and completion of his desire. She is also the first member of that community which together they will create and sustain.

Prior to sin, we are told, man and woman are naked and do not know it. They are without shame. The experience of love is as yet unshadowed; man is ready for a larger exodus from himself, for the perilous journey we call love. Afterward, a cloud no bigger than a man's hand consumes the sun; man and woman, dismayed and despoiled, hide from God. Moreover, man turns upon woman in exasperated judgment; she has led him beyond himself, beyond creaturehood, into *hubris*. God announces a future that goes forward under the sign of conflict—conflict with each other, with the world of nature, with their relationships with Him.

The subsequent chapters of Genesis tell of the dolorous working out of the condemnation. The center breaks apart; the rupture of filial trust in God and each other engenders a family worthy of a Greek tragedy—fear, vanity, division, and murder mark it like a stain. The death of Abel at the hand of his brother is the earthly shape of the war declared on God by man. Man's conflict against heaven has its evil dramatic counterpoint in the unnatural crime of fratricide. Our history of war has begun.

Its consequences spread and spread. At Babel, men lose all power of communication with one another. To the Jews, Babel is Babylon; in the figure of the great temple of the empire, where subject nations are forced to worship idols, the next episode in the human breakup begins. To worship the idols of this world, no matter what terror they inspire, no matter what their arrogance, their total claim on life, is to be struck senseless. As punishment for his idolatry, man is cursed with a poetic, social, and religious impotence.

The myth is particularly ironic. Later in sacred history, the Psalmist excoriates the idolator as a living man who turns in worship to objects of straw and clay and wood. The gods cannot hear or attend or answer those who bend before them. The Babel of many languages is an image of this dead encounter, the prostitution of man before sticks and stones. It is also an image of the inner frenzy and division that corrupt the maker of idols, the worshiper of principalities, the man whose religious life is betrayed and betraying, denied as it is all access to the truth of God. Debased religion, offered up to the masters of empire, extrapolates the inner fury and disunity of men. There is no convergence of praise, no unity of wills, no single voice to speak for men. They talk without sense and listen without understanding. They cry out and no one attends. There is neither compassion on religious truth nor prophecy upon the earth.

The kingdom of Babylon had fallen long before the rise of Christianity. But it is instructive to note how the city arose again, a dream of evil never quite shaken from the consciousness of believers. In John's Revelation, Rome, the new Babylon, is set opposite Jerusalem, as darkness to her light. Rome is the symbol and incarnation of the spirit of malice at work in history, the old enemy in a new guise, seizing on the successive opportunities that human pride and ambition and lust have offered him. The evil one masks his destructive purpose under a specious promise of beatitude, pretending even to be Christ, pretending to be God.

Heinrich Schlier has spoken of the principalities and powers issuing from this kingdom into the world.

> Even the circumstances of history fall under this influence; historical institutions and situations have thus become place and location, means and instruments of those powers. . . . The beast constructs a

political philosophy, an ideology by means of which
the authority of the state permeates everything, es-
tablishes itself, and operates in all places. . . . Satan
can thus take possession of public life by so filling
the persons, means and organs of government with
the will to power, that it inspires them to perform
vicious actions, and invests that spirit with its deadly
effectiveness.

The city of evil and its incarnate powers thus stand in
moral opposition to men of faith, who are their chief op-
ponents in the struggle for possession of the world. The
evangelist John has portrayed the combat with great power,
especially in the thirteenth chapter of the Book of Revelation.

John wrote in the shadow of the corrupt Roman Empire, in the reign of an emperor who had seated himself
in the holy place and claimed the acclamations of the
people as very god.

But judgment is near, as John warns. The oppressed
believers—a handful of shopkeepers, freedmen, and slaves
—are to bring about the overthrow of the empire. Babylon
will fall; the people of God must flee her, for she is cursed.
And the nations at enmity with God will mourn over her
while heaven resounds with praise and gratitude. "She has
fallen, Babylon the great, who of the wine of the wrath of
her immorality has given all the nations to drink."

What could John have meant? Was he expressing merely
the wishful ecstasy of a persecuted, ignorant few who had
recoiled from the world to nourish their fantasies? Or was
something deeper at stake, something that may shed light
on our present world and its technological forms?

A closer look at John's vision will help us decide. For
the seer and his community, the Roman Empire stood for
the apogee of the omnipotent state. And that state appeared to his vision under the most debased of images; it

was simply the beast, the animal par excellence. It is un-
necessary to add that John was not constructing a spiritual
vision that condemned all political power; rather, his beast
symbolizes the repressive, corrupt, and killing form that
power can take when it declares war on the public good
and order. As such, the state is a being devoid of all capacity for conscience and love. Its existence is cut off, in the
nature of things, from communion with persons. It is the
ravening enemy of man, implacably at war with order and
truth. The beast is at once subhuman and superhuman. It
seeks to control human life and to control the natural
universe. So it is able to effect a conspiracy between the
worst instincts of men and the powers of evil that inhabit
"the upper air."

Moreover, the beast is armed with all the faculties of
self-preservation. It claims an arrogant immunity from
death; its power is permeating and self-perpetuating. It
has seven heads to rule the world and ten horned vassals
to protect it. When one head receives a mortal blow, it is
restored; so the beast appears as a horrid parody of the
eternal self-renewal of God. It comes out of the sea, out of
primordial disorder, with no source in God, with no blessing from his hand, a ructation of evil and disorder, to
claim the solid ground of history, the deeds of man. It is
both lettered and literate. It carries on its forehead like an
evil name the blasphemies of those who have given it
divine honors. And from its creator, Satan, it has received
"power, throne, and immense empire."

Against such a power, who could prevail? The evangelist has no illusions. A kind of victory is assured to the
beast, nor merely by its conquests, but by the connivance
of man. "It was allowed to wage war with the saints and
to overcome them. And there was given to it authority
over every tribe, and people, and tongue, and nation. And

all the inhabitants of the earth will worship it"—with one exception only: those whose names have "been written in the book of life of the Lamb who has been slain from the foundation of the world."

But the world is shaken. And so is the community of believers. Many of them fall to worshiping the beast, using the broken phrases of their former worship of God: "Who is like the beast, who could make war against it?"

The vision has the most persuasive inner coherence. The beast, like the Roman world state, is self-sustaining, arrogant, and transcendent. It gathers a pseudocommunity about itself, a court of charlatans and timeservers. The chief of all its crew is a second beast, his identity concealed in the guise of the Lamb. He apes the sacrificial Christ and accomplishes wonders that will lead the faithful astray; the second beast has even risen to life again after receiving a mortal wound. Together with their creator, the dragon, the first and second beast form a kind of anti-Trinity of this world—the father of lies, the misbegotten son, the unholy spirit.

The beast image has a history almost as old as the Bible itself. We are offered in some early traditions an image of creation as a war fought between God and the primordial beast, the incarnation of disorder (Ps. 73:13–14). The first war is placed outside time to give meaning to all subsequent clashes between God and His enemies.

Beasts of the earth, moreover, are at times in the service of God. They execute His judgment against Egypt during the years of captivity. They also act as instruments of God's anger toward the chosen people. Burning serpents sting the faithless in the desert, and in the promised land the locusts devour the harvests.

But the activity of the beasts usually takes the form of war against the divine purpose. Grown implacable and arrogant through long possession of the faithless nations, the beasts finally coalesce into a single enemy of God and man, the beast. He is signed with the power of the dragon, Satan himself. And his final task lies before him. It is nothing less than the assumption of divine power and dominion. His purpose is to claim possession of time and this world; his chief prize is the community of the faithful.

The vision of John catches fire from the events of his own day. And the chief event with which he is forced to deal becomes the first image of his ecstasy. It is the combat between the omnipotent and omnivorous state and the community of faithful.

We have no grounds, of course, for asserting that the vision of John is meant to be applied directly to this or that event, to this or that political regime in history. To think so would be to fall into a crude fundamentalism according to which the word of God is an omnigatherum of human wisdom, freeing man from the burden of judgment upon the times in which he lives. Let us merely say, without taking up larger questions, that the Revelation of John offers us certain immensely powerful operating images, drawn from a definite period of history, elevated and unified by divine truth. The reflective power of believers, operating in the light of faith, is meant to bring the oracles to bear on contemporary life. It goes without saying that men will differ on the application of the vision to any given time and that a great deal of insight and delicacy is needed if the religious lesson once offered is to continue to be useful.

When this has been said, it remains true that there is a substantial religious lesson here for men whose faith requires them to live within their own times and to shed some light upon them. The forces of evil operating around and within us are very great and even overwhelming, John implies. The powers and principalities, of which the beast is the classic incarnation, move like uneasy wraiths in the world; they install themselves in all structures of society. They organize that society, in its climate and affairs, against Christ and God. And in a parallel movement, they exalt civic duty to the point where in some cases opposition to the state, on whatever grounds, is seen as the ultimate crime.

Subversion of the state and corruption of the virtue of patriotism are, however, by no means the only points at which these powers gain entrance into the world. Inhabiting as they do the "upper air," they can even pretend to disappear, the better to infiltrate life, to seed themselves into attitudes, to become spiritually enticing and available. From such a vantage point, there is nothing human which they do not strive to subvert, no institution or movement which is not grist for their jaws. They are immensely skilled in reading the signs of the times in their own favor, in turning human activity to their ends. They can exploit ignorance as well as enlightenment, the forces of stability as well as those of upheaval. And since God's final intervention is sealed against all human prediction, the spirits move with a certain freedom, a breathing space granted them before their day of defeat.

A reflection of Teilhard de Chardin is perhaps of point here:

> A careful observer, studying the earth for a long time from a great height, would see our planet first of all bathed in the blue light of its oxygen; then as time passed, he would see its green vegetation begin to unfold. Then the luminous glow of thought arise within it. But he would also note a shadow, more and more sombre as time passed, and as consciousness grows. The more, indeed, a man becomes

man, the more the problem of evil grows within him; in his flesh, in his nerves, in his spirit; an evil to be comprehended, and an evil to be submitted to.

We have suggested that Scripture offers us little ground for the conclusion that the word of God has spoken of the Roman Empire as evil and has said nothing of any other times. Rather, we must note a double convergence. On the one hand, an empire arose at the time of the early Church, stood against her beginnings, and sought to crush her. But the vision of John is no mere news report. The elevated and mysterious form of the Revelation and the manner in which it is conveyed suggest beyond doubt that its message is panhistorical, with a certain relevance for all time. The Roman experience of the Church thus appears as a single phase of a continuing drama. Throughout history, evil continues to lay claim to the world. The struggle is of massive and constant proportions; it is in fact never done with while time lasts. Men of every period are enticed by forms of evil that the world can neither explain nor evade. Against such evil, believers stand bereft of worldly aid, abandoned to the mercy of God, even subject in a very real sense to the principalities and powers. This is simply our destiny, the meaning of faith lived in the world.

Today, by reason of technology, that faith, lived in the world, offers special complexities. The old order of things is changing so rapidly that man's power of absorption finds itself stretched to the limit. He must live on in a world whose outlines are not at all clear. On one hand, the nation-states are slowly and painfully coming to a realization of human unity. Technology is offering great new opportunities both toward that unity and toward the destruction of all that history has so painfully won. And the religions are undergoing a parallel upheaval. The sacred books, long written, have become for many literally closed books; their primary colors have dated from the pages. In the midst of spectacular human advances in every field, man appears less as a collaborator of God than as His supplanter. The God of Christians even appears archaic and harmless to technological man; He is a father image for the immature, a figure in a remote shrine, which the faithful approach on occasion to leave their offerings. But the tumultuous life of man goes its own way, unaware and profoundly unconcerned. The kingdom of this world is built up and pulled down, only to be rebuilt in a succession of dazzling epiphanies. Designs for world community, inquiries into the nature of life and the sources of the universe—all these seem to assert a lordship once reserved to God Himself. Men of power invite the youthful, those of enterprise and imagination, to move with them into the secrets of the world, to dedicate mind and heart, learning and imagination to the tasks of man. Such a view willingly leaves to God and His worship the old, the disillusioned, the misfits, those whom life has defeated, those who have placed their destiny in a Platonic future with which the living can have only the shortest patience. In the face of a traditional belief in Providence, these men point to the immense, overflowing cornucopia of their own triumphs, to the splendor of their tasks, to the numerous rewards they offer here and now.

Such is, in sketchy form, the critique of divine faith offered by those who hold the keys to the kingdom of this world. It is a notion that one may be tempted to dismiss as contemptuous, pragmatic, and naïve. For men of faith whose lives are led in scenes of urban struggle, in the cold war, in dedication to the world's own tasks, such a critique may seem to have a special and ironic irrelevance. But at least it introduces elements into our understanding that are always lacking when we evaluate our lives from our own viewpoint and sources only. Indeed, the world in which our Savior has lived and died deserves to be heard from; whether we realize it or not, its view of us can be a profound stimulus and purification.

Faith forbids us to disappear into the shrine; the world's sense that faith in God must be relevant to human life is vindicated. But there is a further point to be considered. The world, more exactly the technological world, often asks that faith in itself, faith in progress, faith in time and this world define the boundaries within which the human spirit develops and contributes. And here indeed the lines are drawn. Such a notion of faith—that it rests only in man, in progress, in technology—can never be an acceptable form of divine faith. Men cannot legitimately claim of believers a mode of activity that absorbs their faith in the tasks of this world.

The words of John's Revelation indicate that the struggle is a real one. In the case of the Roman state, the claim of society on man was a present, even a mortal danger. According to the laws of Rome, Christians could continue to survive only at the price of paying a cultic tribute to the state. Which is to say that, in effect, they were forbidden to be Christians at all. John wrote that the beast compels all, "the small and the great, and the rich and the poor, and the free and the bond, to have a mark on their right hand or on their foreheads, and . . . no one may be able to buy or sell, except him who has the mark, either the name of the beast or the number of its name." John is referring to Roman citizenship as it was interpreted under Caesar. Men were compelled to be numbered and "marked" by the state; the assumption was that only in this way could they take their place in civic life and be available to the state in war and peace. But the deepest intent of the masters cannot be ignored. John insists that the tactic of the state is a crude assertion of absolute control over man's life; the faithful, along with other men, are to be marked as beasts in the possession of the beast. The Roman state is determined to lay hold on man's existence for its own ends, to control his political activity, to exact service in its own ends, to control his political activity, to exact service in its wars, to create man's gods and compel submission to them. And it is precisely at this point that a mortal crisis was inevitable for Christians.

For the synagogue and the Church had placed their mark on men, the former in circumcision, the latter in baptism. And each of these marks is a mysterious enrollment in the community of God. Each joins the believer to the covenant of promise; each introduces man to a transcendent hope, a journey whose course leads his life beyond all frontiers of man and into eternity. The man who submits to either of these experiences is marked in a way no human purpose can nullify or deface or eradicate. In a true sense, the believer is now recognizable by God and responsible to Him alone; the mystery of this choice, as the Church Fathers loved to say, places the Christian within the flock, sealed and set aside, irrevocably sacred, untouchable to this world.

When the Christian encounters a form of civil authority such as John knew, a state that claims both conduct and conscience, his reaction must be single-minded, courageous, and publicly evident. Stated simply, the vocation to Christ becomes, in such circumstances, a vocation to martyrdom. For one cannot serve God and Mammon. Believers are forbidden to divide their essential loyalties between this world and the next. Men may be marked as the possession of God or of man, but the mark is in each case a symbol of man's complete gift of himself to another. The mark is evidence of the indivisibility of the Spirit as a gift and the recognition of this by man himself. The mark declares that the existence of man is a gift; to be is to be in service. When the state would seize on mysterious areas of life that belong to God, the believer can never yield. He must die as witness that God exists; he dies too as witness to the truth of human existence.

The issue was clear to the evangelist in the light of his revelation. But the clarity of his understanding and the rigor of his command to the community had another source as well. It lay in the simple claims of the Roman state, which were manifestly and overtly atheistic. Indeed, one of the great benefits that such a state offered to believers was precisely this clear choice. There was no moral vacuum to wander in, no logical corner to hide in, no arrangement or agreement of coexistence possible. The Constantinian peace was far in the future; and by that time, the claims of the state on its citizens had changed radically. But in John's day, the alternatives were clearly drawn.

In our own times, the issues are by no means evident. For one thing, we have no fresh revelation to help us interpret the point at which the powers of this world must be summoned to account. Moreover, the spirit and tradition of dissent, which have always protected believers against absorption by the world, come hard to us. Our religious communities have enjoyed, in the main, centuries of acceptance under the most diverse forms of state power. Christians, especially in the West, have grown skilled in survival; normal times have dulled our edge. A long and honorable life is now the rule for us. Indeed, the rule is so taken for granted by both state and church, so universally presupposed and acted on, that the protesting believer today must almost invariably bear his witness in face of two uncomprehending forces rather than one—that of the state and that of the church. Recent history, in no need of review here, bears this out abundantly.

Such conditions make the task of faith in the world both complex and perplexing. To be able to distinguish—in the midst of all the loyalties that call out to men, in times of war and peace, in times of affluence and grinding poverty, in times of cold war and hot hatreds—the lying presence of the principalities from the true claims of life and love; to distinguish the prophet from the man of destructive rebellion; to discern the point of obedience to God in the command, issued often by the religious authority, to obey man; to see the point of distinction, when it is present, between a call that is holy and one that is sinful; and then to follow, to obey, to stake one's life on a personal vision; to act against all that one may love and cling to and trust in this world; to act on behalf of the Unknown; to stand naked before a jealous God—it is not wonderful that our effort to state the situation of faith is tortured and tentative. For the experience of faith in modern life is infinitely more so.

Our situation allows, of course, for a great variety of response to political institutions. Only a minority of Christians are living under civil regimes which could be called evil, which stand, in principle, opposed to faith in God and to its practice. This being the case, there obviously remains a large middle ground of witness in and through the world, a witness proceeding on the general assumption that one's government is concerned with the common good, including the good of believers. In such cases, an attitude of loving dedication becomes another form of the life of faith in the world. The believer, in such times, can look with patience to an unfolding of history to which he is invited, even urged to contribute. We need not dwell on the themes of the *Triple Revolution* manifesto or of *Pacem in Terris*. Realities of world poverty, of nuclear armaments and conscience, of world community and its hope, the alleviation of disease and ignorance—these are forms of witness in a world we are called to love and sustain.

The word of God announces, to be sure, no single attitude with which to encounter the extremely varied forms of contemporary life. The Revelation of John indicates a very special case, a crisis in political history in which the state has acted beyond its limits. In a clear situation, his vision indicates a clear path. But he by no means intends to legislate ideal forms of political life or to forbid the faithful a part in temporal affairs. Taken in context, John's words set a middle course between two extremes —on the one hand, that of bowing out of the world in the name of moral purity; and on the other, that of paying an unlawful tribute to the systems of this world. Each generation of Christians must, of course, judge for itself how the vision applies to the realities of its own time. What we can be certain of, in a general way, is that the world in any age is a laboratory of the faith in which the conditions of adherence to God are bound to be difficult. In such a world the call to personal and social heroism can never be discounted.

In our own age, as in any other, Christians are summoned to their world, the assumption being that God is serious in placing us in whatever circumstances we must cope with His command to subdue and dominate the world continues to be issued in all seriousness. It goes without saying that in a technological age, the mandate is not adequately fulfilled by submitting oneself or others to primitive circumstances of life, by plowing the ground one's ancestor plowed. Indeed, thinking men have gone beyond such a version of life. It must be added that they have gone beyond any such version of Providence—for themselves or for the world community.

But there remains an opposite view, equally extreme and

unacceptable. What if the will of God, inviting technological man to assume his place in the world as honored
son and collaborator, is seized on as an occasion for activity
of a very different order? What if dominion over nature is
perverted into a new form of the ancient sin, the violation
of covenant, the connivance of human pride with the powers of darkness in war, in racism, in the neglect of the
poor, in the vicious uses of power? The believer must stand
absolutely apart from this enticement; he cannot give himself to such gods.

But such gods are not the true God. The sovereignty of
God, honored by the lawful development of men, stands
free of the destructive power of human pride. The dominion of men over nature, the infiltration of consciousness by
techniques, and the abandonment of faith by the majority
cannot endanger the existence of Him who "wears the
centuries for garments; who sees all things grow old" and
is Himself forever true God. Indeed, God is God. But men
are called to live by faith, and the forms of faith stand
under the fire of time and the scrutiny of men. Faith, by a
paradox as cruel as it is vitalizing, must include new
forms of His Providence, even when the activity of that
Providence seems to recede before the Providential activities
of men, even when God thrusts into the hands of men more
and more responsibility—for peace and unity, for the deprived neighbor, for the well-being of all.

Still, the difficulties of faith go far deeper than these
reflections. Faith must also take into account the new
temptations to revolt and autonomy that technology has
opened. John's vision is significant on this point. New en-
ticements of power almost invariably offer an enticement
away from faith. Man is tempted through his achievements to see himself not merely as growing in human stature but as "like to God." His achievements do not invari-

ably lead him to a stronger sense of sonship—that sense of being a son who grows more like his father, a son who advances from adolescence into manhood. A highly developed sense of power, as Freud realized, tempts man to overthrow his father, to replace him, to build a life without him.

An adult, secure community of sons, on the other hand, reflecting and radiating the intelligence of the Father, responsible for others, conscious of the price of fidelity and of the revenge that unbridled power always exacts in history—could not this be the ideal form of technological community? It would include, as a postulate of man's open nature, an imaginative understanding of the universe, investigation into the nature of life, a sense that every advance of science is indeed a new threshold, a new insight into the Father who invites His sons fully into His household. Such a faith does not attempt to legislate the limits of human inquiry. Rather, it ensures the blessing of Him whose chief glory is man, whose first honor is man's growth in knowledge and love.

The ideal we speak of cannot, of course, be considered as an easy, untroubled achievement. Dealing as it must with world patterns of breakup, crisis, and conflict, faith in God is something more than a tranquil response of man to God's creation. It is much more like the faith of Abraham —an acceptance whose final guarantee carries man beyond the signs of history to His word: "I am God Almighty. Adore me and live."

The modern world, under the sign of technology, has indeed effected an enormously thorough and shattering breakup of the forms of faith into which we were born. Life today has introduced into the modes of faith all the nuances and ironies and complexities that mark life itself. No one who has endured the last thirty years comes to the faith untouched by these fires. Men have sensed during those years the absence of God as well as His presence. They have refused and responded to His Fatherhood, His Providence and Lordship. They have challenged the traditional faith with a faith of their own, often thoughtful and humane—an imperious disbelief. It must also be said that such men, even when they proclaim the death of God, have helped believers to purify their faith of its iron moralism and pietistic absurdities and overcontrol of conscience. Disbelief, by its witness to conscience, has unmasked the clichés of Western godliness and Eastern evil, has urged men of faith toward a more authentic universality. It has awakened in us a sense of the world's poor, amid the spoliation of the arms race. All this evidence, which is the evidence of the way men are living in the mind today and are expressing the life of their mind, is also a ground from which the act of faith may draw an entirely fresh vitality.

The forms of faith today indeed remain hauntingly obscure when we try to summon them concretely before us. What is the will of God for us, singly and in community? What relationships will join human development to the gift of God declared to us in His Son? We have as yet no entirely satisfactory answers; indeed, we are hardly able to forge the right questions. But an awareness of the judgment of men who do not share our belief can be chastening and helpful. Their impatience with religious structures that serve the well-being of an ingroup, that concentrate on possession and control, that are indifferent to suffering and obsessed with pride of place—such impatience is a sign from God that a renewed and purer faith is demanded of us today.

Certain passages from the Book of Isaias are instructive as we seek to become more aware of our future. Four

songs of the prophet depict a perfect disciple of Yahweh
a mysterious servant called by God for a unique task.
Formed by the hand of God and filled with His spirit, the
servant-disciple is destined to restore justice on the earth,
to announce a truth that is both a judgment and a healing.
He fulfills his charge without external show, in gentleness
and, indeed, in apparent defeat. A victim of distrust and
humiliation, he accepts all without failing in heart, for
Yahweh is his support.

The last of the "servant songs" brings this vocation to its
logical and tragic conclusion. The servant is struck down
like a malefactor. His destruction is so logical, so carefully
and justly executed, that it must seem as though Yahweh
Himself stands by the decision of men to remove him
from the earth. But the deepest reality of this life is revealed at the moment of death. His life has not been taken
from him at all; it has been a supreme act of freedom in
the midst of almost universal slavery. The servant has
offered his life for others, for sinners; he has borne their
evil as an intercessor. And Yahweh, in an astonishing act
of intervention, accepts the suffering of His friend as
expiation for all. In death, the servant thus becomes an
epiphany of divine love. The purpose of his life is revealed; it was joined to the loving purpose of God—together they have created and saved the community. Not
only has the servant changed the course of his people's
history, but his sun has mounted into the very heavens; he
has become the "light of the world."

Through the servant figure and his mysterious destiny
the social value of suffering was made explicit for the
first time in history. Under the inspiration of God, the
author of the songs linked the mystery of suffering to the
intercessory power of a just man. And at this genetic meeting of mystery, a light blazes forth. A powerful synthesis is

created; the sacrificial aspect of human life takes on its deepest meaning. In the image of the servant, as a consequence, we have an immensely powerful figure to govern our reflections on the nature of faith. In one man, the author implies, the faith of all the world is concentrated; on him, the experiment of faith in the world, in all its tragic import, has been worked. The uniqueness of the servant does not consist merely in the excellence and constancy of his response to God. It consists also in the way in which faith has organized his life and perfected his attitudes; other men, even good men, cannot match his altruism, cannot launch themselves on the deep. More than this, the life of the suffering servant bears a mysterious social import; it has overflowed in the direction of others. A man has lived and died as God's disciple; his life has been an eminent and even unique service. He has sustained and purified the brethren. Before his advent the community was guilty, and to that extent it was unrecognizable as a family of sons and friends; now the existence of other men has been transformed by one man, who dared and risked all because he believed.

In this man, faith has undergone the entire human adventure. He has spoken and submitted, stood firm and bowed before stress, been heard and weighed, approved and found wanting, won a following and awakened implacable opposition, given himself before the forces of life and death.

Such a man, like the saints of every age, has about him an aura both of mystery and of human attractiveness. He is no gull; he knows life. He is capable of passion; he is aware that the word that was entrusted to him must both form and destroy him—indeed, it must destroy him in order to form him anew. The word of God is within him, not as source of a new, more elevated humanism, in virtue of which he will arrive, by discipline or debate, at a stoic or epicurean excellence. The word of God lies in him as the principle of a new existence; it is a word that creates him anew in and through crisis. It grants him an existence that men will refuse to share; it sets up mysterious vibrations of malice. For the world knows that it cannot remain neutral to this word and remain itself. So the powers and principalities, the masters of the world, move in upon the servant to bring about his destruction.

But he is victorious, ultimately, because he is servant, because he chooses to live and die in service. Service is simply the form his life has taken. As a word is itself only when spoken and available, his life can be understood only in the light of his courageous and long-suffering will to serve, a will that makes of his faith a gift unto death.

Through this man for the first time in history, God has announced suffering and servanthood as preeminent forms of existence in the world. The two vocations are joined by logic and faith. One's will to serve expresses itself in the gesture that enlightens others. But many choose not to hear, and a further step becomes necessary; an ominous tolling sounds in the heart of the servant. He knows obscurely that the word of truth cannot be separated from the spiritual convictions that have engendered it and sent it forth. At the point of crisis, he must stand by his word.

Where he will stand, finally, is in a place of tragedy. The dock, the court, and the scene of execution open before him. They near; he enters on his final hour. And in his deepest anguish and despair, yet another form of suffering appears. For in that hour he stands alone. It is not merely that the community of disciples is absent; they may well be present, but their presence or absence is not the final question. Even a community of men will never substitute for the silence of God.

The good, Kierkegaard tells us flatly, is victorious, but not in time.

We think of men today and of their existence in technological society. And the image of servanthood arises in the midst of our perplexity. It is not a reductive image commanding believers to assume an ordained gesture or role. Rather, it is an image of endless possibility; it offers a generalized attitude toward life, drawn from God's experiment of grace in the world. The image is large enough to encompass every talent, every profession, every state of life. It leads some men to lives of anonymity and others to a great name before men; it urges all, in the name of faith, not to waste their gifts abroad in the pursuit of vanities but to discern the spirits, to refuse to yield before forces of arrogance and fear and despair.

Finally, and in a general way, the image of servant invites us to the acceptance of a minority status in the modern world. It is a form of church that is present to others essentially as a body of service and is determined to serve. Its symbol is the Lord who washes the feet of His disciples, who acts under the sign of the corporal works of mercy, who has come not to be served but to serve, who has urged His disciples to choose the last place rather than the first. And this remains our task, even though other images in history speak of other directions. One thinks, by way of contrast, of the art of the early Roman period representing the Victorious One, risen and ascended, as the ruler of the universe. The art is supremely actual and relevant; it implies the present state of the Lord, His eternal and encompassing kingship. But with respect to us, the image is eventual and relative. It speaks of a victory that cannot be seized on by hands that avoid their own struggle in favor of a victory whose cost they refuse to pay.

The biblical servant chooses the last place and is at

peace there. He prefers moral grandeur to physical power and prestige; he seeks not what is his own, since he sees life as a gift and sees his responsibility as the communication of that gift.

In the world community, we might also add, the servant is in an altogether unique position. As new societies cast off an enforced, white, Western lordship, a servant church can freely take her place in their midst, to show the dignity of a freedom which serves, which is neither white nor black, Jewish nor gentile, but is all things to all men.

It may indeed be true, as Mounier has suggested, that all the centuries of our religious history have been no more than a kind of protohistory of Christianity. Perhaps after all, the servant role is what the Bible has been urging us toward all these years. It may be that we must lose all things before we can grasp "the one thing necessary." The call of Christ does not depend on numbers or power or culture or military resources or the protection and privileges of nationalism. Indeed, these things are disappearing as useful tools of human life. The majority of thinking men are moving in another direction.

And in new society after society, power and its structures are being seized from believers and from their protectors. Western churches and Western societies find themselves before the bar of world conscience—the societies for their crimes of exploitation, war, and enslavement; the churches for having submitted to such regimes, accepted their benefits, and kept silent. Indeed, hardly any future remains today for a community that continues to see its destiny as the extension of such a past—hardly any future in God's plan or in man's regard.

One thing, however, does remain for those whose vision is not enslaved to this world. It is the only thing, after all has been said, that is worth preserving or dwelling on. It is the sublime example of a Lord who binds up and saves, who has poured Himself out, taking the form of a servant. It is the example of One who cannot be finally exiled from this world, since He claims nothing from it except the privilege of being the last and the least of all.